THE SALFORD LANCASTER

<u>ACKNOWLEDGEMENTS</u>

"This book was only made possible because of the help and co-operation given by former 106 Squadron personnel and members of the 'old' community in Salford, as well as friends and families of the crew. Particular thanks to Syd Geater, Peter Perry, Irene Barnes, the men of Manchester Aircrew and Bomber Command Associations and members of St. George's Church. Also Janice, my partner, without whose support it would not have been possible."

Joe Bamford,
October 1996.

THE SALFORD LANCASTER

by

JOE BAMFORD

Pen & Sword Paperbacks
Barnsley

First published in Great Britain in 1996 by

Pen & Sword Paperbacks

an imprint of

Pen & Sword Books Ltd,
47 Church Street,
Barnsley,
South Yorkshire S70 2AS
© Joe Bamford
A CIP record for this book is available from the British Library
ISBN 0 85052 519 5

Typeset by Yorkshire Web,
47 Church Street,
Barnsley, South Yorkshire
Printed in Great Britain by
Redwood Books, Trowbridge, Wilts

Contents

Introduction

During the Second World War 7,377 Avro Lancasters were built and 3,431 of these were lost while flying on operations. On Sunday 30 July, 1944, a Lancaster crashed on the banks of the River Irwell at Salford becoming a statistic along with 246 other bombers recorded as being lost in operational crashes. For the families and friends of the crew it was a day they would never forget. A day when their brothers, husbands and sons were snatched away from them, in an incident that has never been fully explained.

This book is about the seven men who were killed at Salford and the operation from which they were returning when their aircraft crashed. It also covers the period of the crew's operations before the accident, and events on 106 Squadron through the summer of 1944. The crew was typical of the airmen who flew in heavy bombers; a team drawn from different social backgrounds and occupations. They were representative of all those who served in Bomber Command and of the 55,000 airmen who died in its service, many of them from overseas.

As none of the crew survived to tell his tale, I have used accounts and anecdotes of those who flew alongside the airmen killed at Salford. They shared a small but memorable part of their lives together and because of common experiences, are able to describe better than most what it was like to fly on a bomber squadron. Many of the aircrew mentioned in these pages flew on the fateful operation and indeed it could have been any one of their aircraft in pieces on the river-bank and their lives lost. From the recollections of eye-witnesses and official archives the events of this tragic day in Salford's history are told. I explain how a small friendly community coped with a disaster which affected a number of local people for the rest of their lives and is remembered fifty years later.

My earliest memories of this incident date back to the days when as a young boy, I and my father would walk across the ground behind my aunt and uncle's home which stood on Langley Road, near the former factory of Universal Metal Products, onto the banks of the Irwell, from where there is a wonderful view of the Manchester skyline. We used to stand and talk and he often reminisced about things that had happened during the war and significant amongst these memories was the time an aircraft had attempted to make an emergency landing on the playing fields. The aircraft had crashed on its final approach and what remained of the crash site was visible in the form of a large crater, partly filled in but still noticeable. The hole was by then shallow and its shape irregular, the earth having had fifteen or more years to recover from the impact. That crater was the only evidence of the tragedy but today it has disappeared and only memories remain.

My father was in the ARP and on duty until the early hours of the morning of Sunday 30 July, 1944, the day that the bomber crashed. Like so many others he was still in bed, enjoying a lie-in on a Bank Holiday week-end, whereas my grandmother, Lucy Bamford, was downstairs sorting out some washing in the back room. She was badly injured by flying glass and was taken immediately to Salford Royal Hospital where she died two weeks later.

Family gossip about the war and the occasional mention of the air crash may have sparked off my earliest interest in aviation as the Second World War was still a powerful influence during my formative years in the mid-fifties. During the 50s and 60s the war was still a relatively recent event and there was a feeling that we had missed out on the action. Magazines such as *The Air Ace Picture Library* portrayed heroic deeds by airman, with such titles as "Bombers Moon" and "Born To Fly", glorifying air combat and war itself, and these publications probably influenced a whole generation of young men.

By the time I was 14 years old, I had already decided to join the Royal Air Force but my first application for an apprenticeship failed and I was told to re-apply on my seventeenth birthday. My interest in aviation was maintained by frequent visits to Manchester Airport, where I witnessed many changes taking place, as jets replaced older piston engined aircraft like the DC7 and Constellation. One day while I was clearing out a drawer at home, I discovered a fragment of metal. It was a piece of alloy roughly two inches square with a rivet hole in it. Clearly visible were marks to suggest that at some point it had been subjected to intense heat. My father told me that it was a fragment that had blown through his bedroom window when the Lancaster had crashed, and was almost certainly a piece of the aircraft. Having this small fragment in my possession made me more determined to find out as much as I could about the Salford Lancaster.

During my RAF training at Swinderby I visited RAF Scampton for an air experience flight in an Andover. After the flight I was taken around a Lancaster which was sitting by the main gate. It was an early B1 and had the code letters of 83 Squadron on its fuselage: OL- Q for Queenie. The bomber had also flown for part of its operational life with 467 Squadron and previously worn the markings PO - S for Sugar.

With other trainees I stared at the black giant that towered above us and I do not think there was one amongst us who failed to be impressed by its size and design. On the nose beneath the pilot's window, tiny bombs had been painted to indicate the number of operations the Lancaster had flown. Altogether there were 137 of them and although some doubt was cast as to whether it had flown on so many operations, this has now been confirmed. Today Lancaster R 5868 currently wears the markings of 467 Squadron, having been installed in The Royal Air Force Museum at Hendon for many years, where it takes pride of place amongst many other fine exhibits.

The Lancaster that crashed at Salford also bore the letter "S" for Sugar, but the only remaining piece of that aircraft is the small fragment which was blown through my father's window. When it crashed, Lancaster serial number PB 304 was carrying 9,000 lbs of bombs which had been destined for German positions in Normandy before the crew were ordered to abort the operation and return to base. The subsequent explosion was heard eight miles away and widespread damage was reported in all the surrounding areas of Swinton, Pendlebury and Salford.

Apart from my grandmother only one other civilian was killed but at least seventy people were injured badly enough to receive hospital treatment. For one Swinton family, news of the crash caused anguish of a particularly poignant kind. Harold and Dorothy Barnes discovered that their only son Raymond had been a member of the Lancaster's crew and had died less than two miles from his own home in West Drive, Swinton.

Chapter 1

A PROUD HERITAGE

At approximately 1008 hours on the morning of Sunday 30 July, 1944, a heavily laden Lancaster bomber crashed while its pilot was attempting to make an emergency landing on Littleton Road Playing Fields in Salford. Had the accident happened on the moors then few people might ever have heard about it but the fact that the incident occurred in a densely populated area helped to make it common knowledge within a very short while and, reports of it were published in the local and national press. *The Guardian, the Daily Telegraph* and *the Daily Mail* reported the incident although due to wartime censorship restrictions, many details could not be published. There was no mention of the aircraft type, its parent unit or the names of the crew and it was probably because of the lack of official information, that rumours about the crew and their mission quickly began to circulate around the community.

The first concern of most people was to take care of relatives and friends who had been injured. Immediately after the crash, most of the residents in the surrounding area had to clear out their possessions from homes that had been made uninhabitable. Within a few days the affair was brought up in Parliament by Mr Robert Cary, the Member of Parliament for Eccles. He raised the question of compensation and demanded an early reply from The Secretary of State - but the Minister said that the crash was not a unique event and he would have to consult Sir Walter Womersley, The Minister for Pensions. Debate revolved around whether or not the aircraft had crashed as a result of enemy action, but by the end of the week Sir Walter had decided that injuries caused by a British aircraft crashing, were within the definition of "war injuries" and would be covered by the same criteria as if they had resulted from direct enemy action.

Many people have asked the question - why was the pilot of a laden bomber trying to land on a municipal playing field in a built-up residential area like Salford? There is no simple answer and the events of 30 July only make sense if the aircraft's operational role is considered along with the part played by its crew, in relation to the overall requirements of Bomber Command. Most flying accidents did not occur because of any single error or failure, but from a multitude of events that were often beyond the control of individual airmen.

Lancaster serial number PB 304, was on the strength of 106

Squadron and based at Metheringham in Lincolnshire. 106 Squadron was originally formed at Andover in Hampshire on 30 September, 1917. Early in 1918 it was sent to Ireland where it worked as an Army Co-operation Unit, before being disbanded in 1919. The squadron was not reformed until June 1938 when it went into the bomber support role, flying Hawker Hinds for a while, before being re-equipped with Fairey Battles. By the beginning of the war 106 had converted to Handley Page Hampdens, though up to the early part of 1941 it was still only a training unit. After becoming operational the squadron later received Avro Manchesters, before they were withdrawn from service because of the unreliable Rolls-Royce Vulture engines. In the summer of 1942 and while based at Coningsby Lincolnshire, 106 Squadron converted to the Avro Lancaster; a modified and much more reliable four-engined version of the Manchester.

Unlike certain squadrons, 106 at no time received the public acclaim of its more famous contemporaries although throughout the war it maintained high standards and achieved a level of success equal to that of any other in Bomber Command. 44 Squadron was well known because it was the first to fly Lancasters from grass runways at Waddington. Because of the "Dams Raid", 617 Squadron reached a level of fame which exists to the present day. When Wing Commander Guy Gibson was asked to form 617 Squadron, he had just finished his tour of operations with 106 and served as its Commanding Officer for over a year. To form the special unit he took with him three of 106's finest crews, those of Flight Lieutenant Hopgood, Pilot Officer Burpee and Flight Lieutenant David Shannon. Gibson took over as 106 Squadron CO in March 1942 when it was based at Syerston in Nottinghamshire. It did not move to Metheringham until 11 November, 1943, and remained there until it was disbanded in 1946.

Throughout the war 106 Squadron was part of 5 Group, the head-quarters of which was based at Swinderby, near Newark. After the withdrawal of the Manchester, 5 Group was equipped with Lancasters, with the exception of a couple of squadrons which flew Mosquitos as part of the Pathfinder Force. In 1943, 106 took part in the first "shuttle raid" on Friedrichschafen, a tactic adopted to confuse the German defences, in which, instead of the bombers returning to England, they flew on to land at airfields in North Africa. Their target was the Zeppelin Works which manufactured radar sets for aircraft and after completing their mission they landed at Maison Blanche to confuse the Germans who were trying to predict their future whereabouts. This was not the first time Bomber Command had used North African airfields, but it was the first occasion they had been used as part of the overall strategy.

Three nights later the aircraft returned to England bombing La Spezia in Italy on the way home and losing none of the 60 aircraft dispatched. In August 1943, 106 Squadron was in the thick of the action again when it took part in Operation Hydra at Peenemunde, where V2 rockets were being developed. Crews from 5 Group in the last wave of the operation, which involved 596 aircraft, bombed the target using time and distance runs; a new method that was being developed to help crews find the aiming points. Overall the operation was thought to have been a success, putting back the rocket programme by several months; but at a heavy cost to Bomber Command as 40 aircraft including 23 Lancasters were lost.

The seven airmen who made up the crew of PB 304 were a mixed bunch. Six of them had been on 106 Squadron for barely three weeks, but one of them was by the summer of 1944 something of a veteran, having started his operational tour in December 1943. The crew had successfully completed eight operations and crashed on their ninth which was less than the 14 that Churchill's advisor, Lord Charwell, suggested they should complete, and the point at which many airmen saw themselves as being expendable. The airmen aboard PB 304 were not as inexperienced as the records immediately suggest and between them had at least 35 years service. Two were regulars who had served in the Royal Air Force for several years before war broke out and one of those had been involved in six campaigns prior to his death.

The Crew of Lancaster PB 304

Flight Lieutenant Peter Lines --- Pilot

Flying Officer John Harvey Steel ----------------------------- Air Bomber

Flying Officer Harry Reid -- Navigator

Sergeant Raymond Barnes ------------------------------ Flight Engineer

Sergeant John Bruce Davenport ------------------- Mid-Upper Gunner

Sergeant Mohand Singh ------------------------------------- Rear Gunner

Sergeant Arthur Wilmot Young ------------- Wireless Operator/Gunner

After completing their training in the Summer of 1944 the airmen were posted to 106 Squadron at Metheringham. The squadron had recently suffered heavy losses and they were replacing men who had either been killed or taken as prisoners of war during recent raids on underground flying-bomb storage dumps at St Leu d'Esserant. The airfield at Metheringham was built during the winter of 1942-43 on fenland that some claimed was too soft to bear the weight of concrete runways continuously pounded by heavy bombers. It was built to Class A Specifications but when the squadron personnel moved into their new home they found a station barely half-completed and there were many problems with the water and electricity supplies.

Some airmen disliked Metheringham because it was colder and more isolated than Syerston, and being further away from centres of population such as Nottingham - wine, women and song were not as readily available, but they could be found, if one looked in the right places. Most of the accommodation was in the form of Nissen huts, having coke fires which habitually went out, as there was never enough fuel. The nearest village of any size was Martin, a short distance away to the south-east and slightly closer than the village that gave the airfield its name, but this was probably due to the standard RAF practice of naming airfields after the nearest railway station. Many of the crews drank in The Red Lion or The Royal Oak in Martin and both A and B Flights had their own favourite watering holes. Martin generally enjoyed stronger connections with the station than Metheringham and the 106 Squadron Book of Remembrance is kept in The Holy Trinity Church, Martin.

Even by wartime standards Metheringham was a large airfield spread over 11 different sites and was equipped with FIDO, the Fog Intensive Dispersal Operation system which became operational in June 1944. Other aids included the Beam Approach Landing System; an early version of the Instrument Landing System that is still used at most of Britain's airports. Metheringham's main runway headings were 020/200 degrees, giving landing and take-off directions to the north-east and south-west. Living quarters for the WAAFs were situated on Site 9 near the village of Timberlands and the local pub, The Penny Farthing, was a popular venue for airmen with girlfriends living there. The airfield had two type T2 hangars and a single B1 which were situated far apart and the bomb dump was sited to the north, close to Blankey Wood which provided a natural security screen but could be a hazard for aircraft taking-off in a north-easterly direction on runway 02. As was typical of most wartime airfields Metheringham had three runways laid out in a triangular pattern and the main one was 6,000 ft long, the two subsidiary runways being 4,200 ft in length. Its main runway should have been of adequate length for a Lancaster to become airborne, but with a 14,000 lbs bomb load it could sometimes still be a tight squeeze.

In the short time that Flight Lieutenant Lines and his crew were at Metheringham, they would have had few chances to enjoy themselves as they flew nine missions in 16 days. It was a very busy period; the Battle of Normandy was in full swing on the ground and in the air and more daylight operations were flown during this period than at any other time during the war.

Daylight operations were written into aircrew log books in green ink, night operations in red ink and training flights in black. Four out of the nine operations flown by Flight Lieutenant Lines and his crew were "green ink" raids, including the last ill-fated trip to Normandy. This should have been a safer flight than some of their other trips, particularly the operation at Stuttgart two nights earlier when many aircraft failed to return. Some airmen enjoyed flying in the army support role because the operations were different from Bomber Command's normal nocturnal activity and given the right conditions, crews got excellent views of the landing beaches and other sites, including the Mulberry Harbour at Arromanches. The low flying was exhilarating and though there remained an element of danger, the anxiety experienced during daylight raids did not compare with that of the dark nights above Germany. The threat from fighters was drastically reduced and the element of terror, often experienced in the dark, was lifted. The majority of airmen felt more relaxed, but they were still very much aware of the risks.

Chapter 2

THE CREW

After the passage of nearly 50 years it was not a simple task to gather information on seven men who died in 1944. By putting letters into provincial newspapers in the towns where I knew the men once lived, I was fortunate to make contact with several relatives and friends. The Royal Air Force magazine *Air Mail* also helped me out and I had a good response when letters appeared in its pages. Former residents of Langley Road were also extremely helpful and it was a member of the old community who gave me a photograph of Flight Lieutenant Lines the pilot, and also one of the crew. Without those photographs the project would have been much more difficult - if not impossible. The images gave my work a meaning, because I only had to glance at them to be reminded that I was not dealing with fictional characters but the lives of seven real men.

112751 Flight Lieutenant Peter Lines

Peter Lines came from Purley in Surrey, the eldest of three brothers and the son of a manager on Southern Railways. The family home was in Hartley Down, Purley, then a wealthy suburb of south London close to RAF Kenley which during the Battle of Britain was one of the busiest airfields in Fighter Command.

Peter was granted a commission for the emergency as a pilot officer in the Royal Air Force Volunteer Reserve on 1 November, 1941. By the end of 1942 Peter Lines had become an instructor and a pilot of some considerable ability. Flight Lieutenant John Stratford remembered the newly promoted flying officer who arrived on his section of 15 Advanced Flying Unit in January 1943. The unit then based at Acaster Malbis, near York, was equipped with Airspeed Oxfords, a twin-engined aircraft similar in size and design to the Avro Anson. Peter arrived just before 15 AFU moved out of Acaster to the south of England and he would often take an Oxford up and perform aerobatics above the airfield - slow barrel rolls were his speciality and his displays created something of a show; compelling everyone to stop what they were doing and watch the impromptu display.

In late 1943, 15 AFU again moved bases and for a time, Peter and John were based at Damsbury, before moving on to Greenham Common. Their time here was marked by the theft of a road sign which they adopted as a mascot. Appropriately it was an "X" sign marking a cross-road near Greenham Common and one night they lifted it from the ground and drove off with it. From then on wherever "X" Flight went - the road sign went too! On 31 October, 1943, the unit moved to Castle Combe in Wiltshire and Flying Officer Lines headed the movement order. He flew Oxford Serial No X 6853, in the company of Wing Commander J.J. Raino and before the end of the year they were on the move again to Babsdown Farm in Gloucestershire. From Babsdown he and John Stratford separated to commence their training in heavy bombers; after which John ended up on 166 Squadron at Kirmington, another Lancaster - equipped unit under the command of 1 Group.

During the various stages of training Peter never failed to impress instructors with his flying abilities and several of them still have fond memories of him. Flight Lieutenant Stevens of 16 Operational Training Unit remembered him for being good at map reading and instrument flying. Flight Lieutenant Perry, the man who taught him to fly the Lancaster said he had natural skills and knew how to handle an aircraft. Perry was well qualified to judge, having only recently completed a tour of operations with 106 Squadron and flown through one of the worst periods of the war, including the Battle of Berlin. Peter Lines, he said, was one of the finest students he ever taught.

No matter how good a pilot was, before he took command of a crew on operations he had to fly at least one trip as second pilot, a position better known as "Second Dickie". In the early stages of the war pilots had to fly very nearly a whole tour in the co-pilot's seat, but with improved training this changed to a single operation. After leaving behind him the comparative safety of a training base, Peter arrived at Metheringham on 6 July, 1944, and within twenty-four hours was airborne on his first raid.

Flight Lieutenant Lines' initiation to the ways of combat came with an attack on St Leu d'Esserant, targeted at a series of tunnels where flying-bombs were being stored. Lancaster PB 248 took-off at 2245 hours under the command of Warrant Officer Cunningham and for Sergeant Cecil Lawlan, the flight engineer, it would have been an uncomfortable trip; Peter Lines occupying his pull down seat for most of the flight. In the mid-upper turret sat Sergeant Derek Whitehead and in the rear turret, Sergeant Whiting. Over the target many night-fighters were seen and several combats observed as the defences were well prepared for the bomber force which was returning to the target it had attacked three nights before. Warrant Officer Cunningham achieved excellent

7

results that night considering the fierce opposition which successfully intercepted the main force and accounted for 29 Lancasters and 2 Mosquitos.

Out of Jim Cunningham's crew Peter Lines must have been glad to cross the English coast after a night in which they had witnessed many bombers around them going down in flames. German night-fighter crews dropped flares which made their victims more visible and there were rumours that the Germans used "Scarecrow" shells to simulate bombers exploding to promote fear within imaginative minds. Experienced airmen like Jim Cunningham probably knew the truth: that the so called shell bursts were in reality stricken British aircraft manned by their friends and colleagues. Some time after their safe return, Warrant Officer Cunningham discovered that he had lost a good friend that night in Flight Lieutenant Clement who had come all the way from New Zealand to join the fight. It was later learned that his aircraft, JB 642 X for X-ray had crashed in France and all the crew had been killed.

In the relatively short time Peter Lines served in the RAF he rose through the ranks quite quickly. He was promoted to flying officer on 1 October, 1942, prior to his posting to 15 AFU and a year later to flight lieutenant on 1 November, 1943. On 106 Squadron he would have become a Flight Commander within a very short time because of the shortage of those holding his rank. Indeed it is highly likely that another promotion to squadron leader would have followed by the end of his tour of operations.

If he had survived it seems certain that Peter would have been set for a wonderful career in the RAF. He was a man of good education and displayed abounding confidence, making him a popular character amongst his fellow officers.

The Lines family were totally devastated by the loss of their eldest son and Peter's father was extremely unhappy with the circumstances surrounding his death. Peter's mother was keen to make contact with the families of the other airmen. Some months later she took the trouble to travel north and visit the crash site. She called in on local people and left a photograph of Peter and another of his crew with them.

In the 1950s the Lines family emigrated to Canada, where Peter's brothers set up a garage business. His father apparently felt there was no longer any reason to stay in Britain and believed there were better opportunites abroad. Flight Lieutenant Peter Lines' body was never recovered but he is commemorated on The Runnymede Memorial and his name can be found on Panel 202.

542608 Sergeant Raymond Barnes

Raymond Barnes came from a completely different background from that of his skipper. He grew up in the town of Pendlebury in North Manchester; an industrial area with an economy based upon coal and cotton. Raymond was born in Vickers Street and attended St.Anne's Parish Church, where as a young boy he sang in the choir. From an early age he was keen on sport, particularly football.

Raymond's father, Harold, worked at the Wheatsheaf Colliery in Pendlebury and for many years the Barnes family lived in a cottage which was on Bolton Road. Fortunately Raymond did not have to follow in his father's footsteps, but after leaving school became an apprentice joiner with a local company called Gerrards. The firm was one of the biggest joinery construction companies in the region and apprentices received good training and were educated in technical subjects. In the 1930s when most aircraft were built from wood, joiners made the ideal candidates for riggers and his skills would have given him the ideal background to join the Royal Air Force.

On 28 July, 1937, just six days after his 18th birthday, Raymond joined the RAF on an engagement of six years. He first went to Uxbridge in West London to be kitted out and undergo basic training. From there he was posted to number 2 Depot at Henlow on 10 August. After a short stay he moved to Cardington and in November 1937 he was sent to 3 School of Technical Training at Manston in Kent. This was a large training school with facilities for over a 1,000 airmen occupied in a variety of different trades. The young Barnes served at Manston until January 1938, when he returned to Henlow to undertake a flight rigger's course.

On completion of this course, as a fully qualified rigger he was posted to Peterborough where number 7 Flight Training School was based. There he began to develop his skills as a photographer with dramatic effect, as the time when an Airspeed Oxford crashed into a hangar and Raymond was able to capture the scene on film. Peterborough was Raymond's first real posting and from there he went overseas.

At 2.30 pm on 18 March, 1939, Aircraftsman 2nd Class Barnes sailed from Southampton on the Bibby Lines Troopship *Dilwara*. The voyage would take him across the Mediterranean and down the Suez Canal. Before he sailed, he sent a postcard to his parents telling them that he was about to leave: "Dear mother and father," he wrote, "It seems like a big ship and I hope that I am not sea sick. Cheerio for a fortnight!" On his own copy of the same postcard he remarked, "Roll on three years." Little was he to know that his tour would be extended

9

to four years and that his travels would take him to many other countries.

Raymond was posted to 4 Flight Training School at Abu Sueir in the Suez Canal Zone, which by 1939 had been re-equipped with Hawker Harts and Audaxes: two-seater biplanes which were quickly becoming obsolete. The camp was well organized with many sporting and leisure facilities, giving the airmen plenty of opportunities for sand-yachting, swimming and team games. At the outbreak of war in September 1939, 4 FTS was obliged to move across the desert to Iraq, as Abu Sueir had insufficient room for expansion. Instructors and student pilots flew to their new base at Habbaniya, but the ground crews had to travel in rickety old buses on a journey that took three days across Trans-Jordan, Syria and Iraq.

The base at Habbaniya had all the good recreational facilities of those at Abu Sueir - plus a large open-air swimming pool, an open-air cinema and several large messes on the plateau overlooking the main site. In 1940 Raymond took part in the mid-season swimming gala, organized by The RAF Iraq Swimming Association. By this time he had met up with an old friend and neighbour from Pendlebury: Jack Hall. In Pendlebury the Halls had become good friends of the Barnes family, and wrote regularly to Raymond, as well as their own son. Although it is not clear which unit Jack belonged to, he had joined the RAF before Raymond and taken up a ground trade as an engine fitter.

Raymond became a regular member of the 4 FTS swimming team, which went on to win the Iraq Command Gossage Cup. However the amount of time Raymond was spending in the water was affecting his health and as early as May 1940 Raymond spent two weeks in sick-quarters because of an ear infection. However this condition did not prevent him from enjoying his 21st birthday party at an hotel in Baghdad. With Jack Hall, Jack Woolard and one or two other friends, Raymond spent the day drinking and singing along to a banjo played by one of the gang. The party was joined by an Arab Chieftain, who took centre-place when the group photograph, was taken outside the hotel!

But it was not all play. On the flight-line young airmen like Raymond worked hard, servicing ancient biplanes in the hot sunshine, as the shadows of war drew ever nearer to the Middle East. A German inspired revolt threatened the very existence of Habbaniya and all those who served there. It was clear that life in Iraq would never be the same again.

In the spring of 1941 Iraqi forces camped outside the perimeter

10

fence and threatened to shell Habbaniya unless the Commanding Officer surrendered his men. Raschid Ali had overthrown his own government, and had offered the Germans the use of Habbaniya in return for their help to free Iraq of the British. Unfortunately Raschid Ali did not allow for the skill and bravery of a handful of RAF flying instructors, and the determination of everyone on the base to hold out until relief arrived.

The airmen of 4 FTS went to war with a collection of antique aeroplanes, some of which were hastily converted to carry bombs or guns. Audaxes, Oxfords and Fairey Gordons were amongst an odd assortment of aircraft that took part in the battle to save Habbaniya. So few trained aircrew were available that vounteers were used and this was one of the last occasions when someone holding only the lowly rank of leading aircraftsman received permission to fly as aircrew. Ian Martin who lived in the same room as Raymond, flew as observer and air gunner in Audaxes on a variety of sorties; bombing, escorting and patrolling the sky above the airfield. For six days Habbaniya remained under seige with only 39 pilots to defend it. Eventually a DC 2 managed to fly in some relief troops and slowly the balance swung in favour of the RAF.

While this was going on Raymond and his colleagues were kept busy digging trenches to form gun pits for defence, should the Iraqi troops storm the camp. Aircraft flying on raids attacking the enemy had to be turned around in minutes, refuelled, bombed-up and often patched-up as well as could be achieved. As the number of aircraft diminished, the ground crews had to work harder to keep those left airworthy. The battle did not last long but during its time the map of the Middle East changed and 4 FTS was forced to move on.

In July 1941 Raymond joined 127 Squadron: a special unit formed out of "F" Flight of 4 FTS and equipped with four Hawker Hurricanes and four ancient Gloster Gladiators - the biplane which had been the RAF's first metal fighter fitted with an enclosed cockpit. As soon as the Habbaniya siege was over, a new campaign was launched in order to expel Vichy French forces from Syria, and 127 Squadron's aircraft operated in support of "Habforce" which was a task force made up of troops that had liberated Habbaniya, and now found themselves opposing the French. At the end of this campaign, 127 became part of 261 Squadron, which was a unit made up of Hurricanes and also formed at Habbaniya.

Sometime in early 1942, Raymond was posted to India as a result of the transfer of the Habbaniya base from Middle East Command to

11

India Command. He served in Ceylon where there were three main bases at Kandy, Minneriya and Trincomalee on the north-east coast. Raymond had qualified to work on three types of aircraft: the Audax, the Hurricane and the Westland Lysander. All these types are specified on his service record but he may well have had experience of many others, especially in Iraq.

As he returned to England in early 1943, Raymond was lucky to escape when his ship, almost certainly the 21,517 ton *Empress of Canada*, was torpedoed and many of those on board lost at sea. Raymond spent three days hanging onto a piece of driftwood until he got picked up and only his swimming ability and strength saved his life. For weeks afterwards he still had blue dye on his legs from his RAF shorts, which were all he was wearing during his time in the water. After arriving in England, Raymond went on leave before being posted to 75 Maintenance Unit at Wilmslow in South Manchester. Any airman who had served overseas for any length of time was entitled to a posting as near to his home as could be arranged. This was convenient but Raymond had already decided he had had enough of the ground trades and wanted to fly. On 21 May, 1943, he failed his first medical and was classed as unfit for aircrew duties but a month later after a reassessment, he received confirmation that he was fit to fly.

On 13 October, 1943, Raymond began his aircrew training as a flight engineer at 4 School of Technical Training at St Athan in Cardiff. During the course trainees were taken to Woodford where they underwent instruction on the construction of the Avro Lancaster including its electrical, hydraulic and pneumatic systems where they sat an exam as part of their final assessment. Two weeks before his final examination in March 1944, Raymond wrote to his parents telling them what a strain the course had become and, how he was not looking forward to the oral examination. "It's this having to explain by word of mouth that gets me," he told them. "I get tongue tied." Despite his worst fears he passed with a good mark (80%) and was immediately promoted to the rank of temporary sergeant with effect from 20 March, 1944.

Raymond Barnes was slightly built. Indeed when he joined the RAF in 1937 his chest measured only 33" and his height was recorded as a modest 5' 6". What he may have lacked in physical stature he made up for with his personality and people remember his wonderful sense of humour and warm heart. Irene his younger sister recalled the days when he used to send her presents from abroad. The very last time she saw him was during her birthday party on 26 June, 1944, when big brother dropped in to the room to say "Goodbye", bringing with him

12

a present and a card. He said that if he ever flew over the house he would wave a white handkerchief out of the window. This was during Raymond's last leave as he approached the end of his flying training and was about to set off for Syerston and a short course of instruction on the Avro Lancaster.

For his service in the Royal Air Force, Sergeant Raymond Barnes was awarded five medals: The 1939-45 Star; The Africa Star; The France & Germany Star; The Defence Medal; The War Medal. His name can be found on The Runnymede Memorial on Panel 224.

153263 Flying Officer John Harvey Steel

John Harvey Steel was another northener and came from the industrial town of Bradford in Yorkshire. He was the son of Mr and Mrs Samuel Steel living on Fagley Terrace in Eccleshill and attended Hanson School where he became a prefect and eventually was made up to head boy. Mr Ronald Long, who also went to Hanson, knew John very well and confirmed that even as a boy he had a powerful charisma and a pleasant personality. Ronald was younger than his friend, but he got to know and appreciate John for the way he exercised authority in an easy-going manner. At school John's nickname was "Stella" though some boys called him by his middle name Harvey, and after leaving Hanson he went to work in the Treasurer's Office of Bradford Town Council, where he remained for three years before joining the RAF in 1941.

Initially John was categorized as a pilot and commenced training at 4 Initial Training Wing in Scarborough where aircrew cadets were regularly marched up and down the promenade and could easily be distinguished from other recruits by the white band worn around their forage caps. When he completed square bashing he went overseas to America, under the Arnold Scheme, to train as a pilot and prior to setting sail spent a few weeks at Heaton Park near Manchester at the Aircrew Dispatch Centre; close to the place where he was later to die.

John failed to make the grade as a pilot and in RAF language was "washed out" - a not uncommon occurrence since there were many reasons why young airmen failed to make the grade, frequently depending on the number of places available in further stages of training. Some were failed at primary flying school only because the basic flying schools did not have the capacity to deal with the demand. As a result cadets were thrown out for all kinds of reasons - not all of which were connected with their flying ability. A simple breach of discipline or etiquette could be enough to get an individual sent back to Moncton, where airmen were reassessed and categorized in another branch of aircrew.

Having been dispatched to America or Canada for training, cadet airmen rarely returned to Britain until they qualified in an aircrew category of either pilot, navigator or bomb aimer. Those who failed as pilots were often trained as bomb aimers (officially titled Air Bomber). This is not to suggest that all bomb aimers were "washed out" pilots because the majority of aircrew allocated in that trade, were categorized as such prior to them being sent out for training.

Student bomb aimers had to do approximately fifty hours bombing and gunnery practice in Ansons and Fairey Battles. Part of the course involved learning to identify the correct colour of pyrotechnic flares which were used to mark aiming points. The Germans frequently used "spoof" flares to divert the bomb aimer's attention from the real target and on most occasions the only way anyone could tell the difference was by the depth of colour. The Germans never really mastered some colours and this was especially the case with yellow flares. Bomb aimers had to learn how to navigate as it was their job to direct the pilot should anything happen to the primary navigator. Away from the target a bomb aimer's duties also included map reading to confirm the navigator's track or dead reckoning and when visibility allowed, to identify the terrain below.

In the Summer of 1943 on completion of his training, John received a Commission and was promoted to the rank of pilot officer. On his return to England, John, like many airmen returning from training overseas, was sent to 7 Personnel Reception Centre at Harrogate, which consisted of a number of large hotels that had been taken over by the RAF. There he underwent a series of tests and was interviewed by a selection board who decided what command he should be posted to, as the choice for a bomb aimer was quite varied. He could have been sent to either Coastal Command or Middle East Command, but John was selected for Bomber Command and went to begin the final months of his training at an advanced flying school. On 20 February, 1944, he received further promotion to the rank of flying officer.

During the eight operations completed by the crew of PB 304, Flying Officer John Harvey Steel achieved excellent results and was recognized by his senior officers as an enthusiastic and skilful member of the crew. Throughout his service in the RAF he kept in touch with his friend Ronald Long and they met up whenever he went home on leave. On such occasions Ronald was able to give John news of what had been going on at home in his absence and they got to know each other's family well.

On his last leave towards the end of June 1944, John explained to his mother and Ronald that he had experienced a premonition and he did not think he would be returning home again as he was going to be killed. They told him he was being foolish and that his imagination had got the better of him but John was not convinced, and the last time he left his home in Fagley Terrace, he did so with gloomy resignation. This kind of experience was not uncommon amongst those who were about to enter battle and many airmen claimed to have had psychic experiences before or during a difficult moment.

Some years later Ronald Long got married and when his son was born, he gave him the middle name "Harvey" in memory of his old friend. Flying Officer John Harvey Steel is commemorated at The Runnymede Memorial and his name can be found on Panel 209.

J28851 Flying Officer Harry Reid

Harry Reid was one of two Commonwealth aircrew aboard PB 304. He was born in Canada on 24 April, 1921, of Scottish parents. His father, Alexander Reid, was from Kirkwall in the Orkney Isles and his mother, Jeannie (nee Chalmer), had lived on Rousay, an island to the north of the mainland.

Harry was to have a good education and in between passing his high school entrance examination and going to college, he worked for The Eagle Star Shipping Line as a clerk. At The University Of Toronto, Harry read mathematics and physics, but the war prevented him from finishing his degree course and by 1941 he had already served some time in the reserve as a cadet.

On 19 June, 1942, Harry signed on at the Toronto Recruiting Centre and joined The Royal Canadian Air Force for the duration of the emergency. To begin with his university education counted for little and he started off in the ranks as an airman 2nd class. After attending number 6 Initial Training School in Toronto he began his navigation training in March 1943 and just before he became an aircrew cadet, he was promoted to the dizzy heights of leading aircraftsman.

At number 4 Air Observer School in London, Toronto, Harry was introduced to the "Triangle of Velocities" involving such factors as wind direction, airspeed and drift. Other subjects on the syllabus included meteorology, armaments, signals and photographic reconnaissance. The course work was divided up into air work and ground work, each marked out of 1,000 and on completion of his navigation training Harry had accumulated 100 hours on Ansons - a good sixty percent of which was flown at night. Mathematics was an important element for routine calculations and Harry's skills in that area would not have been wasted during the course at London, which lasted nearly six months. On 6 August, 1943, he received his Navigator's Wing.

Having passed out as a sergeant, the following day Harry received his Commission to become Pilot Officer Reid. Almost immediately he was posted to Britain after being given two weeks leave to make his final preparations. On 26 August, 1943, Harry Reid sailed from Halifax, and arrived in England on 1 September, where he was sent to 3 Personnel Recruitment Centre in Bournemouth. Housed in a group of hotels taken over by the Canadians, 3 PRC had just been formed out of RAF Bournemouth under its Commanding Officer, Group Captain Hutchins, OBE. By September 1943, the unit had 387 officers and 1,172 other ranks on its strength: mostly airmen awaiting postings to advanced flying units or operational training units.

Harry languished in this famous seaside town for six weeks until 12 October when he was posted to Headquarters Bomber Command at High Wycombe. It is not known what his role was there but it seems likely that he acted as a liaison officer, performing intelligence or operational duties. He stayed at HQBC only two weeks before returning to 3 PRC and the boredom of awaiting another posting.

In November 1943 Harry started flying training again when he received his posting to number 2 Advanced Flying Unit at Millom in Cumbria. Situated just above Barrow on the west coast and being surrounded by rugged hills, this was not an ideal place for young and inexperienced airmen to further their skills. There were many accidents in the hills around the Peak District and the mountains of North Wales, where training aircraft flew on exercises. Between twenty and thirty hours were flown at AFUs, split between day and night sorties, after which time most navigators were ready to move on to an operational training unit.

Before being posted to OTU Harry went on six days' well earned leave which began on 29 December, 1943, and although it should have ended on 3 January, he was granted an extension of a further seven days by 2 AFU. It seems highly likely that he spent his time celebrating New Year with family in The Orkney Isles and Harry did not return to Millom until 10 January. From there he had a long train journey ahead of him to begin the final stages of training at Upper Heyford near Oxford and he would get no further leave until his course at 16 Operational Training Unit was completed at the end of March. Leave passes in the future would be hard to come by generally, and the

16

prospects of any further trips to Scotland few and far between.

During the war many Canadian airmen served in 6 Group, which began operations in January 1943; sponsored by the Canadian Government 6 Group was almost totally made up of Canadian personnel. 4 Group also had its fair share of Canadians, as did many units in 5 Group. The squadrons that crews were posted to was normally determined by the units at which they trained and many of those from 16 OTU went on to one of 1654, 1660, or 1661 Heavy Conversion Units, to provide replacements for 5 Group. Hence Harry's posting to 106 Squadron.

Education and culture played a great part in the young Canadian's life and listed amongst his hobbies were music and rugby. Harry also enjoyed books and spent many hours reading. Having joined the RCAF knowing that it was quite likely he could be killed or maimed, he must have been committed in his beliefs and keen to partcipate in the war. However Harry did not cross the Atlantic alone and by the end of the war 9,919 Canadian airmen had died. All were volunteers and the fact that they came to Britain so willingly to help the war effort reflects proudly upon Canada as a nation.

Harry was survived by his parents, younger brother George, and his sister-in-law, Grace. She first met Harry and her future husband George, when they were in their teens and all attended the same church in Toronto. It seems that aviation was in the blood of the Reid family and brother George followed Harry into the Royal Canadian Air Force, to train as a pilot before becoming an instructor on Harvards. Having gained his BA and MA in aeronautical engineering, George made a career out of the Air Force, serving for thirty years and reaching the rank of wing commander before he retired at the age of 55. George Reid died in 1993.

At his family's request Harry Reid was buried in the the Orkneys at Kirkwall where his grave is in St.Olave's Churchyard and can be found in Plot 12: Grave Number 10. There are another 129 casualties of war in St.Olaves including another airman from 106 Squadron, whose body was washed ashore there after his Hampden bomber crashed off the coast.

Flying Officer Reid was awarded five medals and a Commendation. They are the 1939-45 Star; The France and Germany Star; The Defence Medal; The Canadian Volunteer Service Medal with clasp; The 1939-45 War Medal. On 12 December, 1945, Harry was posthumously awarded his Royal Canadian Air Force Operational Wings in honour of his distinguished service.

515421 Sergeant John Bruce Thornley Davenport

Sergeant John Davenport was the second oldest airman in the crew, and the one with the longest service in the Royal Air Force. He was 31 years old and had served in the RAF since 2 December, 1931, a total of 13 years. John came from a farming community at Ashley near Market Drayton. Having signed on as a cook and butcher, John commenced his training at Halton and later moved on to 3 School of Technical Training at Manston in Kent. In 1931 the RAF had only a fraction of the number of aeroplanes it would be equipped with during the war years and on its strength were biplanes like the Bulldog, Siskin and Fairey III. Indeed the pay scales matched the size and quality of the aircraft - they were small and out-of-date. An aircraftsman 2nd class in the trade of cook and butcher received approximately £57 a year and in September 1932, when John qualified and was promoted to airman 1st class his pay went up to £68.

For the first two years of his service John worked at Henlow, but in June 1934, he received a posting to Bircham Newton in Norfolk where 207 Squadron were based, equipped with Fairey IIIs. John belonged to the squadron and moved about with it on frequent detachments to the Middle East. In 1935 he left 207 and was posted to the Far East and Singapore, where working in the station headquarters at Seletar he would have seen the comings and goings of the various units which defended this far-flung outpost. This included 205 Squadron which was re-equipping with the Shorts Singapore flying boat whose main duties involved mapping the coast of Malaya and searching the sea for pirates, who still roamed freely at will. He remained in the Far East until November 1936 when his tour expired and a Home Establishment posting came through to 2 Wing at RAF Cosford near Wolverhampton.

While stationed at Cosford, one Saturday night at a dance in Wolverhampton, John met his future wife Irene and in 1939 they were married and set up home in Sedgeley, close to RAF Cosford. During the inter-war years it took many years to move between ranks and by 1939 John was still an airman 1st class - seven years after his last promotion. On 1 December, 1939, he was made up to leading aircraftsman but remained at Cosford until March 1940 when he was posted out to Headquarters 60 Group. Things now happened very quickly for John and by October 1940, he had become a corporal.

In March 1941 he was posted to Hunsdon and received further promotion to the senior NCO rank of flight sergeant, skipping the lower rank of sergeant. When he applied for aircrew duties John was reduced to temporary sergeant - and effectively the rank of airman 2nd class. This was a risk because had he failed to make the grade as an air gunner and not qualified for aircrew there could have been no guarantee that he would be reinstated in his old rank and trade. He arrived at Lords Cricket ground which acted as the Aircrew Reception Centre on 19 July, 1943, and very soon afterwards was sent to Eastchurch on The Isle of Grain to await a posting to an Initial Training Wing. That came through the next month and he spent six weeks at St.Leonards in Sussex drilling, marching and taking a variety of educational courses that the RAF insisted upon. Finally he was sent to Scotland and 2 Air Gunnery School at Dalcross.

Today Dalcross is Inverness Airport, but in 1944 it was an RAF airfield and home of 2 AGS. Wellingtons from 19 OTU at Kinloss regularly used the runways to practise landings and the student gunners would certainly have become familiar with the famous "Wimpy" in which they would later fly themselves. John entered on course number 78 which had 58 trainees. The air gunnery training involved five main elements which varied from beam firing demonstrations to cine cameragun runs. At first each trainee was issued with a single gun and 200 rounds of ammunition, progressing to two guns. At a later stage the student gunners got experience of live air-to-air firing at airborne drogues and approximately 10 hours flying in the single-engined Boulton and Paul Defiant, which as it had a turret fitted behind the cockpit, was ideal as an air gunnery trainer, although it had long since outlived its usefulness as an operational aeroplane. During their air experience gunners learned about the relativity of speed in relation to velocity and angles of deflection. In January John successfully completed his gunnery training and went on leave prior to beginning his flying training at OTU.

John Davenport was a large man who weighed according to one person 15 stone. It is hardly surprising that he operated the mid-upper turret, as certainly his bulk would have made him extremely uncomfortable in the confines of the rear turret. During heavy conversion training he did fly in that position on a number of occasions but after arriving on 106 Squadron he only operated the mid-upper position.

Ronald Hughes, John's nephew, was only a young boy when John perished in the crash at Salford but remembered him by the affectionate name of "Uncle Tubby" - a nickname that aptly described his rather robust appearance. Ronald said that John's wife Irene was so devastated by her husband's death that she devoted the remainder of her life to a career in nursing and never re-married.

At the age of 31, Flight Sergeant Davenport could have sat out the rest of the war in the cookhouse, which many thought to be a "nice cushy number!" We shall never know what made him give up both the security of position and rank, for something which could offer no definite future. Having been in the RAF for so long and seen so much he undoubtedly understood the risks of operational flying.

Sergeant John Davenport is buried in All Saints Churchyard at Sedgeley in Grave Number 19: Row 12.

1324569 Sergeant Mohand Singh

On 8 September, 1941, Mo Singh was called up to serve for the duration of the emergency. He was born in the Punjab, India and grew up in Kamruka in Ludhiana, a town approximately 230 miles northwest of Delhi. Kamruka was an important railway junction trading in wheat and had a population of approximately 52,000 people.

When he was called up Mo was a medical student at a London teaching hospital. He was sent to 11 Air Gunnery School at Andreas on The Isle of Man to course number 2. Although he was slightly reserved, he had a pleasant personality and friendly manner and gained popularity when, as a former medical student he would give lectures on the anatomy of the female body: for the sake of naïve young airmen, who hung onto every word he said!

Number 2 course passed out on 20 November, 1943, and the three airmen who achieved the highest marks were sent straight to a heavy conversion unit which meant missing out on months of additional training at OTU. Mo Singh was one of the three, the other two being Leonard Whitehead and Sergeant Noel. They arrived at 1661 Heavy Conversion Unit Winthorpe but nobody knew what to do with them. As a result they were posted to 1458 Bomber Defence Training Flight at Syerston, where on a three-day course the gunners learned the principle of the "corkscrew" and practised evasion tactics flying in Wellingtons. After that they had a week's leave before returning to Syerston and being given their postings to operational units.

Leonard said he thought Sergeant Noel joined 617 Squadron, while he was posted to 61 Squadron at Skellingthorpe; but until I contacted him in 1990, he had no idea what had happened to his old friend Mr Singh. Why they were posted to operational squadrons with so little training has puzzled Leonard for many years: clearly the omission of five months' further training and flying experience left them in a dangerous position and threatened not only their lives, but also the lives of those who flew with them.

Sergeant Singh was posted to 106 Squadron at Metheringham on 15 December, 1943, and put into the crew of Flying Officer Peter Perry as mid-upper gunner. He and his crew were approaching the end of their tour, and with only seven operations to complete they were an experienced bunch, who had lots of faith in their Lancaster, ND 339 Z for Zebra. This was hardly a good time to begin a tour of operations, as the Battle of Berlin had lowered morale and many airmen felt fatigued but Sergeant Singh was thrown in at the deep end.

Singh's first operation was on 16 December, 1943, to Berlin and it was the first time he had flown at night or above 5,000 ft. Some time after take-off the Sergeant began to complain about his ears, which he said were hurting him. Flying Officer Perry could not turn back so Mo Singh had to suffer in silence and Peter Perry made a mental note that he would have to lay on some extra training at the earliest opportunity.

Lancaster ND 339 Z for Zebra took-off at 1645 hours and above the target area in Berlin the crew observed that the searchlights were quite ineffective, although German night-fighters met the bomber stream over the Dutch coast and near the aiming points where bombs were released at 2010 hours from 21,000 ft. On their return to England many bombers crashed - a large number of bases being shut down in dense fog - and this operation later became known as "Black Thursday". From 106 Squadron, JB 638 flown by Pilot Officer Storey failed to return and altogether 25 Lancasters were lost because of enemy action.

Sergeant Singh's next trip was on 20 December to Frankfurt as part of an operation by some 650 aircraft including 390 Lancasters. The 106 Squadron aircraft left Metheringham at 1710 hours but unfortunately the German Fighter Controller accurately predicted the target and despite a diversionary attack on Mannheim the night-fighters would not be drawn away from the main force. Flying Officer Perry's aircraft bombed at 1945 hours from 20,800 ft, arriving back at Metheringham at 2310 hours. A total of 41 aircraft were lost on this operation.

There were two more raids on Berlin on the nights of 23 and 29 December but Sergeant Singh as part of Flying Officer Perry's crew, was not rostered. They continued training and on 28 December 106 Squadron carried out fighter affiliation exercises with Miles Martinets of 1690 Bomber Defence Training Flight. The next trip for Flying Officer Perry and his crew was a short hop across to Swinderby, where they collected ND 336 P for Poppy, to ferry it back to Metheringham. That aircraft was later lost during the early hours of 30 December on an operation to Berlin.

Nearly two weeks passed before Sergeant Singh gained any more combat experience when his crew took part in another operation, against the inland port of Stettin: thirty miles from the Baltic coast and eighty three miles north-east of Berlin. A diversionary attack on Berlin, by a dozen or so Mosquitos, captured the attention of the Luftwaffe and this raid by 348 Lancasters and 10 Halifaxes was successful. Many industrial buildings were destroyed and several ships were sunk in the port. Altogether 16 aircraft were lost including 14 Lancasters.

There were no major operations between 6-13 January because this was the period of a full moon and the gap was used to provide further practice with the H2s equipment, known as "Y" training. It was not until 14 January that Singh flew again on operations and this time to Brunswick. This was one of the first large scale raids on the city, but the German Fighter Controller predicted the target correctly and the bomber force got badly mauled by night-fighters from the Luftwaffe. 38 aircraft were lost including 11 Pathfinders, as night-fighters penetrated the bomber stream, ND 339 Z for Zebra took-off from Metheringham at 1645 hours and the crew bombed from 22,000 ft at 1915 hours.

Sergeant Singh was in action over Berlin on the night of 27/28 January and survived an operation where 33 Lancasters were lost. The next night the red strip on the briefing map pointed again to Berlin and this was the largest operation in which Sergeant Singh had taken part, involving 677 aircraft. To avoid night-fighters the bombers flew over Northern Denmark, but over Berlin crews experienced strong opposition and 46 aircraft including 20 Lancasters were lost.

There was a long wait now leading up to the crew's final operation and Sergeant Singh must have been wondering what would happen to him when Flying Officer Perry finished his tour. This was another moon period and an opportunity was used to give the weary bomber crews a break. No major operations were carried out between the end of January and mid February.

Berlin had been subjected to another heavy raid on the night of 30 January, involving 534 aircraft; but Flying Officer Perry and his crew were not rostered to fly. On 15 February however 106 Squadron sent 19 Lancasters, its highest number so far, to Berlin as part of a large operation which involved 891 aircraft and Sergeant Singh was part of the crew. Not since the 1,000 bomber raids in 1942 had such a large scale operation taken place. The diversionary raid on Frankfurt-on-Oder failed to draw away the fighters ("spoof" flares were seen close to the main bomber stream) and there was a lot of activity on the run in to the target; but despite the strong fighter presence, Flying Officer Toogood released the bombs at 2118 hours from 22,000 ft.

It was a long flight home but seven hours and twenty five minutes after take-off, Z for Zebra landed safely at Metheringham. Not all crews were so lucky and Pilot Officer Dickinson's Lancaster, JB 534, crashed just outside the airfield boundary at 0010 hours, killing five of its crew. The two gunners ended up in hospital. As Flying Officer Perry's aircraft approached the airfield at 0040 hours, the crew saw the still blazing wreckage and experienced a timely reminder of the dangers that operational flying entailed.

Now that their tour had ended the crew of ND 339 posed for a crew photograph and Peter Perry admitted that prior to their finishing operations several members of his crew would not have their photographs taken, because of superstitious beliefs. He personally, did not believe in such matters and had faith in his own ability and reliance on his aircraft to return them safely. Sergeant Singh stood in the line-up along with the others, despite the fact that many operations lay ahead for him. Flying Officer Forsyth and his crew also completed their tour this night, although they nearly failed to make it. Their Lancaster was struck by an incendiary bomb from another aircraft and they were very lucky to make it back to base.

Throughout the Battle of Berlin 106 Squadron dispatched 280 Lancasters on 20 operations to that city. It lost a total of 8 aircraft and 56 men were killed.

Sergeant Singh never belonged to a regular crew, and after flying with Peter Perry he acted as a spare for any skipper who was short of a gunner. Over the next five months he was to fly with many different crews and very rarely in the same aircraft. On 20 February, he filled in for the crew of JB 612 in a raid on Stuttgart piloted by Flying Officer Fred Mifflin - a young Newfoundlander also destined to die before the end of the war. On 25 February he flew in the same aircraft with Flight Lieutenant Gibbs to Augsburg, made another trip with Gibbs in JB 593 T for Tommy and in late July he flew his penultimate operation in this aircraft.

During the early hours of D-Day, Sergeant Singh was flying with Flying Officer Marchant as part of the huge airborne force that pounded German gun emplacements at St. Pierre du Mont, prior to the Allied landings. After these events he does not appear in the records of 106 Squadron again until 25 July, when he took over from Sergeant Saul. He flew on at least 22 operations including the final one which ended in his death at Salford.

Sergeant Mohand Singh was 27 years old and is commemorated on The Memorial at Golders Green Crematorium in London. His name can be found on Panel 3.

1337510 Sergeant A. Young

Arthur Wilmot Young was born on 26 September, 1923, the son of Wilmot and Beatrice Maud Young, at 30 Maria Street Cardiff. His family was of African-Caribbean origins and had lived in or around Cardiff for many years. His father and two older brothers were merchant seamen and spent most of their time away from home on board ships, so normally he saw little of them particularly after the war began.

Arthur joined up in 1941 and did his basic training at Padgate near Warrington before being posted to Blackpool and number 10 Signals Recruiting Centre, to begin a long and intensive course in the Morse Code and its transmission by wireless telegraphy. It was while he was at Blackpool that he met Jack Atkinson and the two men spent a lot of time together and became the best of friends.

Both young men had a lot in common including the love of jazz music and swimming. Arthur played the trumpet very well, and though Jack owned one, admitted he could hardly play a note: at the height of the big band sound they joined the Blackpool Rhythm Club and regularly attended its meetings. Arthur enjoyed an occasional pint and spent many happy hours in the Tower Ball-Room and at the Derby Road Baths, where he and Jack perfected what they called the "Double Dive". Jack would put his head between Arthur's legs, then turn upside down while holding onto his partner's ankles. So with Arthur standing upright and, while gripping each other's ankles they dived off the high board. Jack claimed that most people thought they were mad! Their antics on the high board gained a rather notorious reputation especially amongst other members of their course.

From Blackpool Arthur went to 2 Radio School at Yatesbury in July 1942 to begin his wireless training; then in March 1943, to the Aircrew Reception Centre in St. John's Wood London. Here many expensive flats had been converted and taken over by the RAF for the accommodation of airmen who slept between six to eight in a room. At "Arcy Tarcy", as it became known, Arthur was kitted-out, read more Morse and did some square-bashing.

The London posting was very popular with Arthur because his friend Jack lived only just down the road in Fulham. He stayed with Jack's family on several occasions and breakfast next morning was normally beans on toast, though despite wartime rationing, Jack's father regularly scrounged extra meat and sausages from a local butcher who was very pro-Royal Air Force and Arthur became quite a popular figure with his family and the neighbours. In illustration of these happier occasions Jack was able to recount a little anecdote about his mother's curiosity. She had not seen many black people before Arthur, and one morning she took him a cup of tea, only to find him still alseep. Looking at his hair on the pillow, Jack's mother thought it had the appearance of wire wool, and the temptation to run her fingers through proved too great–confiding later how great was her surprise to discover its unexpected softness.

Towards the end of March 1943, Arthur moved again to 18 Initial Training Wing at Bridgenorth in Shropshire. At the ITW there were more classes in Morse Code but because of a shortage in the number of permanent staff life was made easier as there was less discipline.

In May, Arthur was again at Yatesbury for a wireless refresher course and this is where he got his first flying experience, in Proctors and Dominies. Trainee wireless operators were taken for flights to get them used to working in the air and the problems associated with it. This course ran until July, when Arthur went to 10 Air Gunnery School on Walney Island.

Sergeant Arthur Wilmot Young was married in his home town of Cardiff on 18 March, 1944, to 20 year old Florence May Silver of 18 Smeaton Street. The ceremony took place at the Church of St.Mary The Virgin, Cardiff. Jack had meanwhile been sent to 13 OTU at Bicester, so he could not stay for very long with Arthur although they did manage a drink together at a club where Jack got to know something more about his friend's family. He discovered that Arthur was the only surviving male member of his family as his father and brothers had been lost at sea, leaving him theoretically at least, to look after his mother and sisters.

Before getting married Arthur had lived at 40 Pomroy Street with his family, including a younger sister, but the couple made their home in Smeaton Street. Jack never saw Arthur again after the wedding - the newly married airman continued his training at OTU, whereas Jack sailed in a convoy from Glasgow to the Far East in May, where he flew in a variety of aircraft including the Dakota. Some years later, he heard that Arthur had been killed in an accident but did not know the details until we met in 1993.

Sergeant Arthur Wilmot Young is commemorated on The Runnymede Memorial on Panel 241.

Chapter 3

OPERATIONAL TRAINING AND CONVERSION

This chapter is about the activity and station life of the units at which the crew of PB 304 lived and trained in the months prior to them joining an operational squadron. Many of the events and incidents do not relate directly to the crew of PB304, although in most cases the men were present at the time they occurred. They have been included to give the reader some idea of the way U/T aircrew were trained in 1944 and a flavour of the intensity of the period.

On 11 April, 1944, six airmen who would soon join Peter Lines' crew arrived at 16 Operational Training Unit, to further their individual skills and flying training. The exception being Sergeant Barnes who as the flight engineer was still completing technical training at St.Athan near Cardiff. So initially the Salford Lancaster crew only consisted of pilot, navigator, bomb aimer, wireless operator and two air gunners.

Based at Upper Heyford in Oxfordshire, 16 OTU was equipped with the Vickers Wellington twin-engined bomber, most of which had seen better days on operational squadrons. The Wellington had been built for two-pilot operations and did not have a position for a flight engineer and neither did it have a mid-upper turret, only beam guns. Flown by day and night on continuous exercises by trainee airmen, the airframes and engines of the aircraft were pushed to their design limits.

Before the airmen began flying training, they had to be formed into crews and this ritual was normally carried out in a hangar or on a parade ground, where new arrivals were given a certain amount of time to sort themselves out. Much has been written about the informal way that airmen met up with those to whom they were about to entrust their lives, but each man's experience was different. Pilots seeking a competent navigator might meet a bomb aimer, who would say, "I know just the chap you're looking for!" Men in similar aircrew categories such as air gunners, sometimes stuck together hoping to join the same crew; airmen milled around, looking for familiar faces, a smile or other gesture that might signify an invitation. It was all a bit of a lottery - but for the majority the system worked.

In many cases it was not only faces airmen looked at, but medal ribbons, badges of rank and other obvious signs of operational experience: one former air gunner I spoke to said that to begin with he crewed up with a young inexperienced pilot, but during a conversation with a flight lieutenant he learned that the officer had been a flying instructor and was short of a gunner. Thinking that the officer's experience as a pilot might be a key factor in keeping him alive, he opted to leave his sergeant and join the flight lieutenant's crew. It was a wise choice and the crew survived a tour with 149 Squadron in 3 Group.

However not everyone had the luxury of deciding who they should fly with and one former navigator who joined the RAF in 1941 was put into a crew only after attempting to fail an examination and get back-flighted. After returning from Canada on the *Queen Mary* and on completion of his training as a navigator he and a friend were posted to 6 AFS at Staverton and subsequently to 19 OTU at Kinloss. For some reason they arrived later than the other student navigators and found that all of them had already been crewed up. The two men decided that as they were surplus to requirements, they should deliberately fail an examination, since this would mean they would be sent home on leave and return for the next intake a couple of weeks later.

Soon they both received a message to attend the Flight Office, and thought their devious plan had worked - but were soon disappointed. The Flight Commander informed them that they had both passed the examination with good marks - better in fact than some of the navigators who had arrived before them! So they would now take their places. Almost immediately two pilots walked in and claimed them as their replacement navigators. Both crews got through tours of operations in 4 Group.

Sergeant Syd Geater who later joined 106 Squadron at Metheringham and flew on operations alongside the crew of PB 304 decided that he would choose his pilot, rather than be chosen. During a cold November morning parade in greatcoats, at Upper Heyford, he was looking around and saw three smiling, friendly types who turned out to be Canadians. Former Flying Officer Mitchell best described what happened next in a letter to Syd in 1991: "We were standing outside a permanent type building down by the control or headquarters area and were supposed to choose a wireless operator from amongst 20 or so lads mingling together. It was agreed by the three of us (myself, Don and Bill) that we wanted the best and would not rush into this decision. Then it happened - this "Pip Squeak" of a sergeant wireless operator comes charging out of the group, smartly salutes, and in his very confident manner, advises us with no uncertainty, that he is our wireless operator and we need look no further!" Syd sealed the deal by inviting the officers to the sergeants' mess for drinks and this was allowed as a one-off occasion.

Getting as far as OTU and becoming part of a crew was a major stage in an airman's training; but for some this experience turned sour: the death of a pilot and crew greatly affecting those who were left behind. Such events were an ever-present consequence of wartime operations resulting in enforced changes to the regular crew manning a particular aircraft. For example an air gunner might stay behind for ground instruction, or a navigator become temporarily replaced when repeating a particular element of his training. If a pilot failed to return, or his crew were badly injured, it left individual airmen in an unenviable and isolated position.

Many airmen whose crews were killed, or too badly injured to continue flying, had to go back to the beginning of training and re-enlist with another crew. If this happened in the early stages of OTU, it might not be so bad, but the psychological effect of losing colleagues one was just getting to know, could be potentially devastating. To lose a crew during the second part of operational training at heavy conversion unit stage could be a very severe blow: an airman had often to return to OTU and start all over again.

Sergeant Stan Goodman who flew with 106 Squadron's Commanding Officer lost his crew when they were killed in an accident at 17 OTU Silverstone, but he had stayed on the ground that day and so found himself in this simultaneously lifesaving but deprived situation. Rather than send Sergeant Goodman back down the training line, someone made the sensible decision to allow him to continue to the HCU and he was put into the crew of Wing Commander Piercy who was just beginning his second tour and about to take command of 106.

The reasons why airmen were impelled together as a team are difficult to explain and rarely bear close examination. Peter Lines' crew consisted of amongst others, an accountant, a physics graduate, an armature winder, a cook and at a later stage a joiner. The chances are that none of them really knew much about each other, unless they shared a room in the officers' or sergeants' mess and the element of anonymity may have helped the system to work. Having three officers in the crew, met the requirements and approval of The Aircrew Selection Board, who considered the categories of pilot, navigator and bomb aimer the more demanding, and should be filled by those airmen holding The King's Commission. The fact that it took two years to train a wireless operator/air gunner must have failed to capture the Board's attention.

We can only speculate on how Flight Lieutenant Peter Lines and his crew got together at Upper Heyford, but a pilot with Lines' amount of experience would have attracted attention and stood out from U/T pilots. Certainly Sergeant John Davenport had been in the service long enough to know how the system worked and be aware of the perils that lay ahead with an untrained pilot. Peter Lines' background may have been different from that of his fellow officers while he was looking for those with similar interests to his for the two key positions of navigator and bomb aimer. On operational stations, those officers or senior NCOs who were in the same crew, often shared the same room, and they would not want to end up lumbered with someone with whom they had nothing in common. Flying Officer Reid, like Lines, who enjoyed squash and tennis, was a bit of a sportsman and had other things in common. Flying Officer Steel fitted in because he had had a good education and leadership qualities which were also important in a crew. He also had some flying experience. For the NCOs it may have been fitting that Sergeant Arthur Young ended up in a crew with an older man such as John Davenport, who like himself was also married. Having lost his own father, he may have found the experienced 31 year old gunner a man with whom he could easily get on. Sergeant Robert Saul was 35 and the oldest man in the crew and like Sergeant Davenport, he lived in the Midlands at West Waddon.

Flight Lieutenant Lines and his crew entered on course number 73 and were assigned to "B" Flight. One of the staff instructors who worked with them and remembered Lines was Flight Lieutenant Stevens. He was particulalrly impressed by Peter's skill at flying on instruments but knew that as a former instructor himself, it was always likely that he would exhibit better than average ability. Peter's course had two other former instructors on it, namely Flight Lieutenants Scott and Bellasco. Pilots and navigators completed approximtely 100 hours of flying at OTU, of which 40 hours had to be performed at night. The total number of student airmen at 16 OTU in January 1944, were 34 pilots, 32 navigators, 30 bomb aimers, 28 wireless operator/air gunners, and 58 air gunners. Each intake had between 14 and 16 pilots.

When they arrived at an OTU the vast majority of airmen had never flown anything larger than the twin-engined Anson and their experience of team work was quite limited. At this stage of training they learned to co-ordinate with other members of their crew by passing on information, learning to accept the advice of others, and generally helping out if required. The rear gunner, Sergeant Robert Saul, was the "eyes" of the aircraft, occupying a position to defend it against sudden attack from behind or below and Miles Martinets of the bomber defence training flight attempted to sneak up underneath the Wellingtons at night to test out the gunners' reactions. If they got close enough without being spotted, the Martinet pilot switched on his landing light to simulate firing his guns and by then it was too late for evasive action.

During the early stages of training, pilots learned to fly by visual means and contact with datum points on the ground. Their reliance upon instruments was confined to an altimeter, compass and air speed indicator, but at OTU Pilots were trained to rely on instruments, so that they could fly safely through cloud and bad weather without becoming disorientated. The Link Trainer was a ground-based aid which allowed pilots to practise this realistically, where under a darkened hood, the simulated cockpit gave pilots some experience of night-flying's dependency on a turn-and-bank indicator and the gyros. In effect, the trainer was an early version of the modern flight simulator, in which pilots spent a minimum of six hours under the hood; and even with his accumulated experience Flight Lieutenant Lines would not have avoided it.

To help improve airmens' technical knowledge of the aircraft and the components upon which they relied, visits were arranged and Peter Lines and his crew would have gone to the Vickers Factory at Weybridge and to Airscrews Ltd, who manufactured propellers. Flying training involved many risks and during the war more than 5,000 men were killed in flying accidents. Some crashes happened because of mechanical failure and problems beyond control of the pilot, while others could unfortunately be blamed on bad airmanship and negligence.

In early February 1944, three accidents occurred at 16 OTU in two days. On 2 February Wellington BK 454 departed on a night cross-country and bombing exercise during which, shortly after take-off the rpm on both engines surged rapidly to over 3,300; and at the same time the aircraft's intercom broke down. The pilot, Flying Officer McMurdy, orbited in a left-hand circuit and tried to sort the problem out, but failed to stop the engines from surging. The young pilot then committed himself to a landing, which he carried out successfully, but both engines were so badly damaged that they had to be changed.

Next day LN 400 crashed on take-off killing four airmen; a few hours later Wellington DF 616 made a belly landing because the student pilot forgot to put the wheels down. There happened to be an instructor on board the aircraft who failed to notice a bright red light glowing on the instrument panel and this unfortunate man was given a reprimand and an endorsement to his rating.

Towards the end of their OTU training, crews sometimes flew on diversionary or back-up missions, such as mine-laying, and during the period Flight Lieutenant Lines and his crew were at Upper Heyford, 16 OTU were involved in two such operations, on the nights of 21/22 January and 1/2 March. The January raid involved 8 Wellingtons mine-laying at St Nazaire but it is unlikely that the Lines' crew took part as they were only a month into their course. However it is possible they flew on the March raid, though the OTU records are not as detailed as those of the squadrons and this cannot be confirmed.

With so many exercises having to be flown, the airmen were put under a lot of pressure, which in turn added to the risks. In addition to the flying, crews underwent ground instruction and the syllabus made for a long day, with the morning flying briefing being held at 0730 hours and the night-flying briefing beginning at 1400 hours, followed by the second detail who had their briefing at 1630 hours. The day finished with a final briefing held at 2230 hours. Before they left the OTU, airmen had to go into the decompression chamber, where their bodies were subjected to the atmospheric conditions experienced at an altitude of 20,000 ft. This prepared them physically for future flights at altitude.

Neither Flight Lieutenant Lines nor any member of his crew were recorded in the Operational Record Book of 16 OTU because nothing out of the ordinary happened to them, since normally only those who had accidents or were involved in misdemeanours got a mention. Many others like the Lines' crew, did manage to complete the flying programme without incident and during the second week in April they finished their course.

After reporting to Winthorpe on 11 April the airmen were immediately posted to the 52 Base Aircrew Combat School at Scampton where they had to learn and practise survival and evasion tactics. The course was normally concluded with an evasion exercise, when airmen were dropped off many miles from camp and then had to find their own way back, opposed by the military, the police and other forces who endeavoured to capture them. As this course was not widely popular cheating was a common practice and all kinds of "dodges" were used by trainees to allow them to make a safe return.

Flight Lieutenant Lines and his men were then posted to 1661 Heavy Conversion Unit at Winthorpe near Newark on 6 May. Twin-engined bombers had been replaced by four-engined "heavies" at most HCUs as early as 1942, when the Short Stirling had been introduced into service. By 1944 however the Stirling was obsolete in the bombing role and equipped many of the HCUs: the Lancasters having been sent back to operational squadrons in January. It is probably fair to say that the Stirling was the least popular of the three main types of four-engined bombers, because compared to the Lancaster and Halifax, its ceiling of about 14,000 ft was too low: making them more vulnerable to anti-aircraft guns.

Sergeant Barnes was crewed up with the others at Winthorpe, having arrived at 1661 HCU on 1 April, a fortnight before the rest of the crew. It is pure speculation as to how he became part of the team but Raymond Barnes had spent a considerable amount of time in Cardiff since October 1943 and knew the city well, having also been posted there many years before. There is evidence to suggest he may have known Arthur Young and visited his home in Pomroy Street.

The Commanding Officer of 51 Base, Wing Commander Jennings, was concerned about the safety of his crews because the Americans were regularly infringing his airspace with low-flying Dakotas and USAAF bombers. In May 1944, this became something of a problem, as the American aircrews were breaching agreed safety regulations: flying at heights below 1,000 ft and posing a hazard to those on operational training throughout the area. Winthorpe, and Syerston were particularly affected but despite a strong letter of protest from Squadron Leader Hyem, to the Commanding General of the United States Tactical Air Force, the low flying continued. For crews learning to fly four-engined Stirlings, there were enough problems to cope with and unauthorized activity in the circuit constituted a real threat.

The strength of 51 Base during this period was 2,500 students and 1,900 permanent staff: a considerably larger establishment than that at OTU. The training syllabus demanded the courses be split into two different groups; so that on one day the first group would be flying and the second group attending lectures in the classroom. The next day they would change roles. The flying began with general handling and familiarization exercises, an instructor sat in the right hand seat, since unlike the Lancaster, the Stirling had been designed to be flown by two pilots and the spare seat was normally occupied by staff.

On the occasion that Flight Lieutenant Lines and his crew took their first flight, there were probably anxious moments all round, as the huge aircraft slowly wound its way from the dispersal to the threshold of Winthorpe's 6,000 ft runway. Lining the bomber up on runway 22, under the guidance of his instructor, Flight Lieutenant Lines carried out final checks, running the engines to 2,000 rpm against the brakes. When the brakes were released, he pushed the throttles foward, led with the two starboard engines to avoid a swing to the right caused by torque. As speed increased he pushed the control column forward to lift the tail and lateral direction then depended on the use of its huge rudder. With the Stirling lumbering off the ground, the brakes were applied and the wheels retracted. As the undercarriage went up the Stirling became tail-heavy and could not be fully trimmed-out until the flaps were raised, but thereafter when they were safely airborne, the rest of the crew could breathe a sigh of relief until it was time to land.

As flight engineer, the main role of Sergeant Barnes, was to monitor the temperature gauges and look for any signs of "Coring" when oil passing through the radiator congealed, causing circulation problems and overheating of the engine. The flight engineer also kept a keen eye on the fuel gauges and logged the fuel as it was burned off, as the gauges were known to be inaccurate. At Winthorpe the Stirlings used only 87 Octane fuel as opposed to the 100 Octane they had carried on operations. Lower Octane fuel allowed the engines to produce the same rpm but less boost, as the aircraft carried far lighter loads than it had been built for on operations and additional power was not required.

Landing a Stirling could be quite a dodgy business, especially in a cross-wind, due to the large surface areas of its tail and undercarriage, which caused the bomber to float sideways in the slightest breeze. Several accidents happened while Flight Lieutenant Lines' crew trained at Winthorpe and though some were minor incidents, others had more serious consequences. On 17 May EE 956 crashed near Rothwell in Northamptonshire, killing all nine crew and since this accident occurred at night it was thought to have been caused by icing. On 7 June EH 940 caught fire and dived into the ground at Kettlethorpe. Only two airmen survived the crash.

Some instructors played cruel tricks on their students to ensure they did not make the same mistake twice. One former staff flight engineer said he had a student who failed to notice the most obvious things that were wrong, and on one exercise the instructor waited until the aircraft was landing, then quickly slipped the fuse for the undercarriage into his pocket. When the wheels failed to go down, he waited for his student to check the fuses, but he forgot and so had to wind them down manually. On the early Stirlings it could take eight minutes or more of back breaking labour to wind the gear down - and up to fifteen minutes to retract it! It also involved an elaborate procedure after landing, to reset the undercarriage for electrical operation. The former instructor

33

remembered his student was not a happy man when he returned the fuse on the ground – but he certainly learned his lesson – the hard way.

Former wireless operator, Flying Officer Vic Cuttle, who flew on 106 Squadron at the same time as Peter Lines and his crew, recalled that not all crews passed through HCU intact and both the bomb aimer and navigator in his were replaced at Winthorpe. Mr Cuttle was never sure why this happened but thinks that they must have failed to make the grade for some reason. On 31 March, 1944, and with Flight Lieutenant A.L. Williams at the controls, he and his crew were lucky to escape when their aircraft overshot on landing. The Stirling ended up on its nose and several of those on board received minor injuries. A few weeks later the bomber was back in the air but it crashed again at Farsley near Leeds killing a single member of another crew. In June 1944, aircraft from 51 Base were involved in a total of twelve accidents, three of them concerning crews of 1661 HCU.

During the second week in June, Flight Lieutenant Lines and his crew were approaching the end of their training and preparing for the final exercise. This was normally a long four or five hour flight, incorporating a bombing and cross-country exercise, which on some squadrons were known as "mufflers" and on occasions would take the Stirlings dangerously close to the French coast, so that the crews could become familiar with visual references on the shoreline. With the completion of this last trip the seven airmen would be allowed some leave and then posted to 5 Lancaster Finishing School at Syerston.

Flight Lieutenant Lines' crew were given six days' leave on 20 June and this was almost certainly the last time any of them saw their families and friends. At 5 Lancaster Finishing School they were put under the supervision of Flight Lieutenant Peter Perry, who had completed his tour on 106 Squadron in February. He had since been awarded the Distinguished Flying Cross and promoted from the rank of flying officer. Each instructor normally had three crews under his control and Flight Lieutenant Perry at this time also supervised those of Flying Officer Garlick and Flying Officer Pockner.

When they arrived at Syerston most crews had approximately forty hours of flying time on the Stirling and initially they were given instruction on the Lancaster's airframe; followed by fifteen hours flying experience, of which half would be solo. Most courses lasted up to two weeks, but with demand for aircrew at its peak, five crews were put through by special order in a matter of days and Flight Lieutenant Lines' crew was one of them.

On 28 June, the crew went on their first flight in a Lancaster and the airmen would have experienced the problems of climbing over the main spar for the first time. This obstacle was bad enough to negotiate on the ground, but in flight with the bomber dipping and yawing, it could be very difficult. The first exercise was flown in R 5912, RC - L for Love and Flight Lieutenant Lines' first detail was to carry out circuits and bumps, later supported by familiarization and asymmetric flying on three engines.

Peter Perry said that once they were airborne it was obvious Flight Lieutenant Lines knew how to control the Lancaster, so he changed his plan and showed him a number of manoeuvres instead: some of which he called "tricks". This was something he had not done with a student before, but thought it a waste of time going through procedures which his student already understood and this initial flight was therefore quite a long one, lasting some two hours and thirty minutes.

The next day Peter Lines was airborne again in Lancaster Mark 3, ED 578 G for George. Exercise 2 would normally have been solo circuits and landings but Flight Lieutenant Perry decided to skip these and go straight to Exercise 3, which involved dual evasive actions, corkscrewing, diving turns, banking searches and fighter affiliation. The gunners would have practised the corkscrew repeatedly on the ground and now had the opportunity to put it into practice in the air. Pitting their wits against the Martinet pilots of 1690 Bomber Defence Training Flight, the gunners had to warn their skipper of any intended attacks and in turn he would give a running commentary on his actions. The pilot would call: "Down port - changing - up port - changing - rolling - up starboard - changing - down starboard - rolling - down port - changing". This continued either until the hostile aircraft disappeared or to the point when the pilot no longer had the strength to struggle with the controls.

On board the Lancaster were several devices that enabled early detection of fighters. One of these was called "Monica", and as the wireless operator it would have been the duty of Sergeant Young to monitor the radar based system. Monica later became unpopular with some pilots because its use often involved a lot of chatter between the gunners and wireless operator. The intercom was a vital channel of communications and pilots feared it could block out other essential messages. Monica had only a limited capability anyway and outside its operating funnel, fighters could still remain undetected and attack from blind spots behind and underneath the bombers.

The penultimate exercise at 5 LFS took place on the night of 30 June in W 5008 F for Freddie involving another two hours of circuits and

35

touch and go landings - to give Peter Lines the feel of the Lancaster and get used to handling the bomber in the dark. Normal practice at this stage immediately after tuition required the trainee pilot to fly his first solo, if he had not already done so. Peter Perry recalled that, either because of the weather or the aircraft going unserviceable, Flight Lieutenant Lines did not fly his solo circuits and bumps this night; resulting in the exercise being abandoned and continued the following evening. Safety was a key factor.

In July 1944, 5 Lancaster Finishing School completed its second month and 2,000 hours of flying without an accident. To some extent this was to be expected, as when the crews arrived at the unit, they were becoming experienced airmen and had the capability to sort out their own problems as they arose. 5 LFS was still part of 51 Base and its Headquarters Staff at Swinderby were complaining in June that flying control at its airfields were not forwarding take-off and landing times to HQ. Without this information they did not know when an aircraft had become overdue and it also made it more difficult to allocate aircraft and control the daily flying programme.

Flight Lieutenant Lines flew his final exercise at 5 LFS during the evening of 1 July, and this took the form of a forty-five minute check flight in R 5668 O for Orange. The previous night's detail having already enabled Lines to complete his preliminaries, he now flew solo to the satisfaction of Peter Perry. Not all the crew were on board on this occasion: only Flying Officer Reid the navigator, Sergeant Young the wireless operator and Sergeant Barnes the engineer. The final exercise under normal circumstances was number 7, involving a two hour cross-country and a "Bullseye" bombing competition carried out on purpose-built ranges at Bassingham or Fenton. Because of the unusual programme of this course no practice had been arranged.

Having been pushed through 5 LFS in four days, the five crews were not urgently required by 5 Group after all. So with their flying training now complete Flight Lieutenant Lines and his men had to hang around and wait for their posting to an operational squadron, although their time would have been put to good use undergoing ground instruction including dinghy drill. The dry drill was practised on an old Lancaster fuselage section and when this had been completed they were taken to Nottingham Baths for the wet dinghy drill. On 6 July, Flight Lieutenant Lines and his crew were posted to 106 Squadron at Metheringham. During the month of June the squadron had lost seven aircraft.

Chapter 4

ESPRIT DE CORPS

In July 1944, 106 Squadron was the only unit to be based at Metheringham when the station was commanded by Group Captain McKechnie who was an efficient and popular officer who looked after the welfare of his crews. The Commanding Officer of 106 Squadron was Wing Commander Piercy, who had taken over from Wing Commander Baxter DFC on 13 March, 1944. Baxter had been respected amongst those in the ranks, but Piercy did not enjoy the same level of popularity. A position of command is often remote from those who come under its control and different men handle situations in different ways. Wing Commander Piercy may not have been well liked by all the airmen on 106, but his own crew thought him to be a good pilot and he enjoyed their mutual respect.

On 7 July, the day after Flight Lieutenant Lines and his crew arrived at Metheringham, Air Commodore A.C.H. Sharp visited the station as Commander of 54 Base which included Coningsby, Woodhall Spa and Metheringham. Although the airfield and its facilities were under the control of Bomber Command, the USAAF had recently begun to use it to evacuate wounded army personnel. Casualties were transported by road from nearby Nocton Hall Military Hospital, to be flown to Prestwick in Dakotas, prior to repatriation to the United States. This caused a few problems with the catering arrangements and dispersal of the aircraft. It is not known why Metheringham was chosen for this role, but it was probably connected with the fact that it was equipped for Fog Intensive Dispersal Operations. FIDO airfields had pipes containing petrol laid down the side of the runway and in bad visibility these were ignited. The intensive fire burned away fog and mist. Metheringham may also have been used because it was conveniently situated close to Nocton Hall.

A cricket match also took place this day between Metheringham and Woodhall Spa. The previous day Metheringham had beaten Coningsby by 13 runs, however their luck ran out in the 5 Group knockout competition when they, the home side, were beaten. Woodhall had Flying Officer Stanford from 617 Squadron playing for them, an Australian State team cricketer with something of a reputation and when he was run out for only 5, things looked good; but Metheringham's score of 67 was later easily passed by Woodhall, who still had wickets in hand. That these matches were played during a period of such intense activity says something for the spirit of wartime airmen and their determination to carry on their lives as normally as possible.

Sergeant Geater and his crew arrived at Metheringham on 16 June, a little under a month before those who would later fly in the Salford Lancaster. It is interesting to note that one of the aircraft that his crew flew in during their working up period was Lancaster serial number ED 906, a survivor from the dams raid of May 1943. The aircraft then coded AJ - J, had been flown by Flight Lieutenant David Shannon DFC, himself a former 106 Squadron pilot prior to the formation of 617 Squadron. With Flying Officer Don Merideth as pilot at the controls, Syd flew in the veteran bomber on three occasion, carrying out checks during circuits and landings. The crew could not fly on operations until their pilot had made at least one operational flight with an experienced pilot and crew, when he would observe what went on as a second pilot.

Flying Officer Merideth flew his second dickie trip during the night of 18/19 June on an operation to Watten and after take-off the rest of the crew went to the pub, anxious for his safe return. A short time later they heard the familiar sound of Merlin engines overhead and soon the equally familiar and smiling face of Don Merideth appeared round the door, to confirm that the main force had received a recall signal shortly after crossing the English coast outbound. Because he had crossed the coast it was considered that he had completed his first mission and that they were now eligible for operations, although this would not happen immediately.

On the night of 4/5 July, 106 Squadron flew on operations to St Leu d'Esserant to attack underground storage dumps housing flying bombs, so that Syd and his crew found themselves on the Order of Battle for the first time as part of a 231 strong force of Lancasters from 5 Group. On their first operation the crew performed very well and according to the bomb plot (Number 440), the bombs from Flight Lieutenant Merideth's aircraft landed only a short distance to the north of the aiming point - in fact only Flying Officer Kitto from 106 Squadron bombed closer to the aiming point than Fying Officer Merideth's crew.

Two Lancasters from 106 were lost on this operation: ME 832 flown by Flight Lieutenant Futcher and ND 339 under the command of Flying Officer Crosier. Six of Futcher's crew were killed and only Flight Sergeant McNaughton, the bomb aimer, survived and evaded capture. Their Lancaster was attacked by two enemy fighters which set the bomber's engines on fire causing it to go into a spin; and although the gunners shot down one of the fighters it was too late to save their aircraft. Crosier's aircraft also went down after being attacked by a fighter, crashing at Bellencombre in France. Flying Officer Crosier, who had joined the squadron in March was an experienced pilot. He was killed but four of his crew survived to become evaders, their two less fortunate colleagues being taken as prisoners of war.

Flying Officer Mavaut's aircraft ND 682 came under attack from a fighter and he had to make an emergency landing at Woodbridge, but the bomber was badly shot up and the mid-upper gunner had died by the time it landed. For Flying Officer Merideth's crew in LL 953 C for Charlie, the operation went as planned and nothing more than what had been expected and prepared for was encountered.

Arriving at Metheringham in between two operations on St Leu d'Esserant, Flight Lieutenant Lines could hardly have unpacked his bags before he was assigned as second pilot to Warrant Officer Jim Cunningham; as 106 Squadron prepared to send 16 of its Lancasters to form part of a force of 208 aircraft from 5 Group.

106 SQUADRON ORDER OF BATTLE

Battle Order	Captain	A/C Serial No	ID Letter
1.	F/O Durrant	JB 663	A
2.	F/O Mather	ME 789	B
3.	F/O Merideth	LL 953	C
4.	W/O Cunningham *(F/Lt Lines 2nd pilot)*	PB 248	E
5.	F/O Mavaut	PB 191	H
6.	F/O Kitto	LM 215	F
7.	F/Lt Marchant	ME 668	L
8.	F/Lt Williams A G	PB 284	U
9.	P/O Pemberton	ME 778	O
10.	S/Ldr Marshall	PB 144	P
11.	P/O Monaghan	ME 831	R
12.	P/O Thompson C E	JB 593	T
13.	F/O Harris	LL 948	V
14.	F/Lt Clement	JB 641	X
15.	P/O Thompson	PB 122	Y
16.	P/O Kipfer	LM 221	Z

There were two reasons why former Warrant Officer Jim Cunningham remembered the night when he had Flight Lieutenant

Lines as his second pilot. It was the night when 106 Squadron suffered its heaviest losses and the night he also lost a good friend. Warrant Officer Cunningham had joined the RAF in March 1942 and learned to fly on Tiger Moths at 15 Elementary Flying School Carlisle, followed by further training at 28 EFTS Wolverhampton in 1942. His rear gunner, Sergeant Whiting, claimed that Jim Cunningham only became their pilot after the first one was taken out of training - apparently because his legs were too short to reach the rudder pedals so resulting in his transfer to another Command. When he joined 106 Squadron on 19 February, 1944, Jim Cunningham held the rank of flight sergeant and underwent his 'second dickie' exercise with a Flying Officer Latham the same night that he arrived, during a sortie on Leipzig. Latham had made his first trip with the then, Flying Officer Peter Perry, the pilot who instructed Flight Lieutenant Lines to fly the Lancaster at 5 Lancaster Finishing School.

For the operation on 7/8 July the bomb load was 13,000 lbs (11 x 1,000 lb + 4 x 500 lb) and the fuel volume 1,500 gallons. PB 248 took-off at 2245 and as usual the main force was to route out via Reading to position 5030N 0020W, where it would split up into three, where half the force was to take route one, while the remainder was divided to follow two other tracks.

Night-fighters of the Luftwaffe were extremely active, especially on the central route where 24 aircraft were lost, and Syd Geater recalled that his crew, flying in LL 953 C for Charlie, witnessed their first combat close to the French coast. As they neared the target the number of combats increased and became so regular that his pilot and navigator agreed not to log any more actions, but noted that Flying Officer Mitchell, the bomb aimer, opened fire from the front turret on one night- fighter that got too close. It was not seen again and after bombing at 0121 hours from 12,000 ft all thoughts were put into their survival and getting back to base safely. At 0119 hours the controller, Wing Commander Porter, lost his VHF radio and the Deputy Controller, Squadron Leader Eggins, automatically took over, until 0125 hours when the he ordered all crews to cease bombing.

Sergeant Whiting, the rear gunner in Warrant Officer Cunningham's crew pointed out that because his position was very remote, his only means of communication was through the intercom. He could hear Flight Sergeant Hovey, the navigator, giving his skipper compass bearings and Jim Cunningham always told the crew when they were leaving the British coast and approaching the coast of France. It was a three-and-a-half-hour flight to the target and Sergeant Knight the bomb aimer released PB 248's bombs at 0120 hours from 13,000 ft; achieving impact only 120 yards from the aiming point. The return flight was much quicker and Flight Lieutenant Lines with Warrant Officer Cunningham almost certainly at the controls, touched down at 0250 hours.

Either at the debriefing session with the intelligence officers, or more likely through conversation amongst ground crews, the airmen realized that a number of aircraft were missing. In fact, 5 Lancasters failed to return to Metheringham making this a black night for 106 Squadron. Warrant Officer Cunningham's friend, Flight Lieutenant Clement, flying JB 641 X for X-ray was one of the many victims, his aircraft crashing at Quetteville where only two bodies were found and buried at St Sever Rouen. Flight Lieutenant Clement had been on the squadron since February 1944.

ME 668 flown by Flight Lieutenant Marchant was probably hit by a fighter and the starboard inner engine caught fire, causing the entire Lancaster to burst into flames. Marchant gave the order to abandon the aircaft but being wounded in the leg he asked for help to get out, which was fortunately forthcoming enabling three of the crew to survive including Marchant and the flight engineer. The bodies of the navigator, mid-upper gunner and rear gunner were buried at Aunay near Dienx but that of the wireless operator was never found. Pilot Officer Monaghan's crew were luckier in that they all survived after ME 831 was shot down by two fighters: five of the crew evading capture and two being taken as POWs. Squadron Leader Marshall's aircraft, PB 144, was shot down by flak at 0130 hours resulting in all the crew being killed and they are buried at Mirissel near Beauvais and St Geneive. Flying Officer Mather's aircraft, ME 789, was also shot down by a fighter at 0100 hours but all its crew survived although six were taken prisoner. Flying Officer Evans the navigator, evaded capture and returned to England on 30 August. Altogether 29 Lancasters and 2 Mosquitos were lost that night.

Warrant Officer Cunningham was a fiery able Scotsman who loved flying and the excitement that went with it, but he was also a man who liked a little fun in the sergeant' mess and did not always appreciate the intervention of authority. On one occasion Wing Commander Piercy refused to sign his leave pass, so without hesitation Cunningham went over to the Station Commander's office and spoke to his fellow countryman, Group Captain McKechnie, who agreed he should have the leave and rang up Piercy, telling him to sign it. On Cunningham's return to the Squadron Commander's office, Piercy was livid and a huge argument broke out; afterwards ensuring that the two men never got on and avoided each other as much as possible.

Not every senior NCO or officer could knock on the group captain's door and get his problems dealt with in this way, but Warrant Officer Cunningham had earned the respect of many senior officers as a result of his part in a very daring raid on the night of 10/11 June, 1944, when he and his crew in the company of nine others from 106 Squadron, bombed a railway siding at Orleans in France from 600 ft. The train was carrying a panzer division on its way to reinforce the German line in Normandy and it was vital that it should be destroyed. For Flight Sergeant Archer it must have been quite exciting as he was on his first trip as second pilot. On his return the warrant officer was informed that His Majesty The King had awarded him an immediate DFC, which honour gave him certain privileges incuding (apparently) that of arguing successfully with his Commanding Officer. The recommendation originated from Bomber Command Headquarters.

Sergeant Goodman, Wing Commander Piercy's rear gunner, had great admiration for his skipper, encouraging an entry in his log book which read: "Wing Commander Piercy, a pilot who knew how to treat a crew!" They had joined 106 Squadron in March and flown their first operation on 19 March to Stuttgart and like most crews had a favourite aircraft, in their case ND 682 K for King. Sergeant Goodman only had one disagreement with his wing commander and that was when he removed him from the rear turret and put him in the mid-upper position on 29 June for a daylight raid on Beauvais. Wing Commander Piercy had done this to give another airman the necessary experience for promotion to warrant officer and although this angered Sergeant Goodman at the time, he subsequently valued his tour with the wing commander.

It was within this environment of anxiety and personal conflict that Flight Lieutenant Lines and his crew found themselves in early July. Because most 5 Group squadrons were rested after the operation on 7/8 July when so many aircraft had been lost, new crews were able to put in some further flying training before going on their first trip, as for example on 11 July, when a blind bombing exercise was held involving the usual air to sea firing off Skegness. At some time during the morning of 14 July, however, the seven airmen wandered into the offices of "B" Flight, up behind the control tower, where on the notice board they would see their names listed in second place on the Order of Battle for operations later that evening. If they had not already done so each airman would have made out his Last Will and Testament, as a part of a routine because the chances of them being killed were quite high. Sergeant Raymond Barnes signed and dated his this particular day and it had already been signed and witnessed by Sergeant John Davenport, the mid-upper gunner, and a D. Young of 40 Pomroy Street Cardiff. This was Sergeant Arthur Young's home address and suggests that the flight engineer and air gunner had paid a visit to his home during their final leave at the end of June.

Now they were about to fly their first operation the airmen would have had to get into the routine that preceded every raid and for some airmen this was something of a ritual. The first stage was briefing, normally held about two hours before take-off, when details of the operation were given by various specialist officers. After the final order came the well known words, "Gentlemen will you please synchronize your watches!" If they were hungry the airmen could now visit the mess, for a pre-flight meal of eggs and bacon. After that it was into the flying changing lockers where airmen divested themselves of personal possessions and the gunners put on their Kapoks, with a canvas outer suit containing electrical heating. When they were dressed in flying clothing it was off to the parachute store behind the control tower and the ritual neared its end as the crews either walked, or travelled by bus and lorry to the dispersal. On arriving at the aircraft each member of the crew had his own pre-flight checks to carry out and kept busy until after the engines had been started and warmed up. The engines were then shut down and crews had to wait for the signal to start engines again - a period of inactivity which most airmen considered the most difficult to bear, as by now they were keen to get airborne and on with the operation.

Operation 1: 14/15 July Villeneuve-St George.

The target: marshalling yards close to Paris which had been attacked by Bomber Command several times before and 106 Squadron dispatched 10 Lancasters out of a total force of 242 aircraft, from which 128 were to attack Villeneuve whilst the remainder were to bomb other marshalling yards at Revigny. Flight Lieutenant Lines and his crew flew in PB 298 B for Baker which was normally flown by the crew of Squadron Leader A.L. Williams, but they were on leave. PB 298 was listed number 2 in the Order of Battle and loaded with 9,000 lbs of bombs (18 x 500 lb). Flight Lieutenant Parry AFC was a new arrival on the squadron and flying his first operation as second pilot with Flying Officer C.E. Thompson.

106 SQUADRON ORDER OF BATTLE
Operation 1: 14/15 July Villeneuve-St George.

Battle Order	Captain	A/C Serial No	ID Letter
1.	F/O Durrant	JB 663	A
2.	F/Lt Lines	PB 298	B
3.	F/O Kitto	LM 215	F
4.	Sgt Bumford	PB 281	J
5.	F/Lt Stewart	PB 203	M
6.	F/O Rabone	LM 641	P
7.	F/O Thompson C E *(F/Lt Parry 2nd Pilot)*	JB 593	T
8.	F/Sgt Archer	PB 284	U
9.	F/O Fyson	PB 122	Y
10.	F/O Kipfer	LM 211	Z

PB 298 took-off at 2215 hours and routed via Bridport to position 4915N 0255W. To begin with the bombers flew as one force but Lancasters attacking Revigny broke off at 4750N 0000. The time allocated over the aiming point at Villeneuve was between 0127 hours to 0145 hours; time over France 2346 hours to 0259 hours and whilst crews encountered thin layers of cloud, visibility was generally good. PB 298 bombed slightly late due to some problems with the marking of the target but Flying Officer Steel released the bombs from 6,000 ft at 0150 hours, aimed at red and green Target Indicators. No results were observed but an aiming point photograph was taken.

The bombers on the Villeneuve raid were not plotted accurately by the German fighter controllers, although some activity took place near St.Malo when an Me 109 was claimed as being destoyed at 0143 hours, and there was another combat near Tours between 0233 hours and 0237 hours. Some crews experienced heavy flak, but light flak was also intense and accurate west of the target. 7 Lancasters were lost on the Revigny operation.

106 Squadron Lancasters dropped a total of 160 x 500 lb GP bombs and 18 x 500 lb MC with 72 hour delay fuses. On Flight Sergeant Archer's Aircraft, PB 284 U for Uncle, two 500 lb bombs hung up and were returned to Metheringham. Altogether six aiming point photos were brought back and the general opinion was that the operation had been successful, PB 298 landing at 0505 hours.

The following night 106 Squadron again attacked the railway system at Nevers, led by Wing Commander Piercy, but Flight Lieutenant Lines and his crew were stood down.

Operation 2: 18 July German Troop Positions

For their second operation Flight Lieutenant Lines' crew were given a brand new Lancaster, fresh off the production line at Woodford and this was to become their regular aircraft. PB 304 was given the squadron code letter "S" as part of "B" Flight whose aircraft bore the code letters from "L" to "Z" inclusive.

This operation was part of the greater battle for control of the Normandy battlefield and a prelude to OPERATION GOODWOOD. Under the command of General O'Connor's VIII Corps, three armoured divisions were to attack the German line whilst the job of the bombers was to flatten any opposition thereby creating a corridor through which Allied forces could advance. 106 Squadron's part in this was to target the Mondville steelworks which had been turned into a fortress by the defending German forces. 19 Lancasters were dispatched towards a total of 942 aircraft, including 667 Lancasters and the Order of Battle was headed by Wing Commander Piercy. PB 304 took-off at 0415 hours and its weapon load was 13,000 lbs (11 x 1,000 lb + 4 x 500 lb).

106 SQUADRON ORDER OF BATTLE
Operation 2: 18 July German Troop Positions

Battle Order	Captain	A/C Serial No	ID Letter
1.	W/Cdr Piercy	PB 203	M
2.	G/Capt McKechnie	PB 303	R
3.	S/Ldr Williams A L	PB 298	B
4.	F/O Browne	LL 953	C
5.	F/Lt Jones	LM 215	F
6.	F/O Boivin	ND 331	G
7.	F/Lt Taylor	PB 191	H
8.	Sgt Bumford	PB 281	J
9.	F/Sgt Netherwood	PB 145	L
10.	F/Lt Stewart	PB 248	E
11.	F/Lt Williams A G	PB 232	N
12.	F/O Harris	ME 778	O
13.	F/O Rabone	LM 641	P
14.	F/Lt Lines	PB 304	S
15.	F/O Thompson C E	JB 593	T
16.	P/O Thompson J G	PB 284	U
17.	F/Sgt Archer	PB 296	X
18.	F/O Fyson	PB 122	Y
19.	F/O Kipfer	LM 211	Z

Group Captain McKechnie was flying with Warrant Officer Cunningham's crew as Cunningham himself was ill. Originally Flying Oficer Durrant had been listed to fly, but for some reason he was scrubbed and replaced by the group captain.

The main force attacked in three waves. Time over the target was between 0603 hours and 0607 hours and Flying Officer Steel dropped PB 304's bombs at 0606 hours from 7,500 ft, noting that they fell in a concentrated pattern close to the steelworks and all the crews identified the areas to be attacked near the canal docks. Ground defences were light, no fighters were seen and the biggest danger on this operation came from bombs being dropped by those aircraft flying at a higher altitude. One Halifax crashed after completing its bombing run on the steelworks and it is thought it had been hit on its starboard fin and rudder by bombs from another aircraft.

A total of 6 aircraft, including a single Lancaster, were lost after being damaged by flak, sixteen aiming points photographs were obtained and units of Panzer Group West sustained confirmed damage. Flying Offcer Fyson's aircraft PB 122, had a 1,000 lb and a 500 lb bomb hang up and Flying Officer Kipfer in LM 211, also had a 500 lb bomb remain in its racks but all these were returned safely to base. PB 304 landed at 0740 hours.

As in many previous battles the Germans quickly regrouped, in sufficient strength to slow down the Allied advance. Over 400 British tanks were destroyed by 88mm flak guns which doubled up as anti-tank guns, whilst Tiger tanks also accounted for much of the destruction. The 11th Armoured Division lost 126 tanks, in one day alone and the much needed breakout was again halted.

After Bomber Command left the target, aircraft of the USAAF visited the area and dropped another 2,000 tons of bombs, making a total of 6,800 tons. During the day 18 aircraft of 106 Squadron were detailed for an operation that evening at Revigny but they were stood down at 1800 hours and the airmen of 106 Squadron were fortunate not to have taken part in this operation; since of the 115 Lancasters from 5 Group which attacked Revigny, 24 were lost, amounting to 21% of the force. This was largely due to the German fighter controller plotting them early: the Northern France Running Control Centre passing on plots of aircraft flying south of London between 2330 to 2349, as they approached Gravesend. 15 Me 110s of III/NJ5 were sent to the Cambrai area at midnight, and the time over target was extended until 0140 hours. 619 Squadron based at Dunholme Lodge lost 5 Lancasters on this unhappy night.

46

Operation 3: 19 July Thiverny

17 Lancasters from 106 Squadron took part in this operation against a flying-bomb launch and storage site, twenty five miles north-west of Paris, which had been attacked a week earlier by aircraft from 4, 6 and 8 Group. On that occasion cloud had prevented the target being effectively damaged and this operation was now to be carried out solely by Lancasters and Mosquitos of 5 and 8 Groups. The promotion stakes were prominently in view during these momentous times as evidenced by Flight Sergeant Archer's commissioning in the rank of flying officer, coupled with Pilot Officer J.G. Thompson's promotion to flying officer.

106 SQUADRON ORDER OF BATTLE
Operation 3: 19 July Thiverny

Battle Order	Captain	A/C Serial No	ID Letter
1.	F/O Durrant	JB 663	A
2.	F/O Browne	LL 953	C
3.	F/Lt Stewart	PB 248	E
4.	F/Lt Jones	LM 215	F
5.	F/O Boivin	ND 331	G
6.	Sgt Bumford	PB 281	J
7.	F/Sgt Netherwood	PB 145	L
8.	F/O Mavaut	PB 203	M
9.	F/O Marks	ME 778	O
10.	F/O Rabone	LM 641	P
11.	F/Lt Parry	PB 303	R
12.	F/Lt Lines	PB 304	S
13.	F/O Thompson C E	JB 593	T
14.	F/O Thompson J G	PB 284	U
15.	F/O Archer	PB 296	X
16.	F/O Fyson	PB 122	Y
17.	F/O Paterson	LM 211	Z

PB 304 took-off at 1925 hours loaded with 13,000 lbs of bombs (11 x 1,000 lb + 4 x 500 lb). The aiming point was identified visually and the bombs released at 2131 hours from 15,000 ft. Altogether twelve Lancasters from 106 bombed visually, three more bombed onto red Target Indicators and the remaining two onto yellow. The red TIs were not correctly placed on the aiming point and generally the bombing was somewhat scattered - heavy flak being moderate but accurate and resulting in damage to two 106 Squadron Lancasters. Flying Officer Mavaut's aircraft, PB 203 ZN - M was hit at 17,500 ft and, PB 303 ZN - R flown by Flight Lieutenant Parry, at 17,000 ft, but despite being severely damaged both aircraft returned safely to Metheringham and no fighters were seen.

A good aiming point photograph was brought back which shows clearly the flying-bomb launching ramps and puffs of black smoke from exploding bombs. Flight Lieutenant Lines reported that the bombs from PB 304 fell in a concentrated pattern around the aiming point - no aircraft were lost and PB 304 returned to Metheringham at 2335 hours.

Wing Commander Guy Gibson, VC, flew on this raid with Squadron Leader Miller from 630 Squadron at East Kirby in LE - N. This was one of Gibson's last flights in a Lancaster, as he argued to get back on operations. After this date he mainly flew Mosquitos and Lightnings, until his death on 19 September, 1944.

Operation 4: 20/21 July Courtrai

The weather on this Thursday was warm and an inter-section crick-et match took place between "A" and "B" Flights. The latter were bowled out for 56 and looked to be beaten. "A" Flight very sure of themselves - unaccountably scored a mere 36 runs however and in allowing themselves to be defeated came in for a lot of verbal abuse! Many of the players later found themselves rostered for this operation and 106 Squadron contributed 20 Lancasters to a total force of 317 aircraft, which included 15 Mosquitos. Following Air Vice-Marshal Cochrane's policy that all pilots should be officers, Sergeant Bumford had recently been commissioned and made up to the rank of flying officer.

106 SQUADRON ORDER OF BATTLE
Operation 4: 20/21 July Courtrai

Battle Order	Captain	A/C Serial No	ID Letter
1.	F/O Durrant	JB 663	A
2.	F/O Mavaut	PB 203	M
3.	F/O Browne	LL 953	C
4.	F/O Sayeau	PD 214	D
5.	F /Lt Stewart	PB 248	E
6.	F/Lt Jones	LM 215	F
7.	F/O Boivin	ND 331	G
8.	F/Lt Taylor	PB 191	H

Battle Order	Captain	A/C Serial No	ID Letter
9.	F/O Bumford	PB 281	J
10.	F/Sgt Netherwood	PB 145	L
11.	W/O Cunningham	PB 298	B
12.	F/Lt Williams A G	PB 232	N
13.	F/O Harris	ME 778	O
14.	F/O Rabone	LM 641	P
15.	F/Lt Lines	PB 304	S
16.	F/Lt Parry	PB 303	R
17.	F/O Thompson C E	JB 593	T
18.	F/O Archer	PB 296	X
19.	F/O Fyson	PB 122	Y
20.	F/O Paterson	LM 211	Z

This was another late night raid on marshalling yards and PB 304 took-off from Metheringham at 2315 hours loaded with a 13,000 lbs bomb load. The routing to the target was via Orfordness to 5130N 0318E - 5057N 0330E - Courtrai. The time over the target was between 0055 hours and 0101 hours; time above Belgium 0043 hours to 0116 hours. Flying Officer Steel released PB 304's bombs at 0057 hours from 12,000 ft, but unfortunately a single 500 lb MC bomb hung up in PB 304's bomb racks, compelling Flight Lieutenant Lines to fly out over the North Sea and it was jettisoned in position 5116N 0220E at 0110 hours from 11,000 ft. Altogether, on that night 106 Squadron dropped a total of 116 tons of bombs, to establish a new record for 5 Group on a single night.

It is claimed that the target was totally destroyed and only 9 Lancasters were lost on the Courtrai operation, although another 28 aircraft were lost on raids at Bottrop and Homberg. There were no searchlights over the target but heavy flak was effective and as the bombers turned for home the fighters moved in to pursue the force out over the North Sea. Gunners in Flying Officer Paterson's crew flying LM 211, claimed to have shot down a twin-engined fighter that was seen to hit the ground and other action included a foray by a Mosquito, which shot down an Me 110 after a ten minute chase. The Mosquito was damaged and its crew later baled out over England. PB 304 landed safely at Metheringham at 0210 hours.

Amongst the 4 aircraft lost from 5 Group was Lancaster PD 205 piloted by Flying Officer Garlick of 9 Squadron, who had been one of the three airmen under the supervision of Flight Lieutenant Perry on

Flight Lieutenant Lines' course at 5 LFS. His operational service had lasted less than three weeks.

Sunday 23 July

Metheringham was visited by Wing Commander Wooley, Wing Commander Brown and Wing Commander Wilkinson, all from 5 Group Headquarters when another cricket match took place between the officers and senior NCOs - the officers making 105 for only 5 wickets then bowling out the senior NCOs for just 48 runs. During these endeavours Warrant Officer Cunningham ferried PB 232 to Woodbridge and returned in his beloved "Queenie" which had been at the emergency landing ground since being damaged while he had been on leave.

During the evening 106 Squadron dispatched 12 Lancasters to bomb Kiel, but Flight Lieutenant Lines and his crew were not on the Order of Battle. A total of 629 aircraft attacked Kiel including 519 Lancasters and the force arrived behind a "Mandrel" screen which jammed the German radar, culminating in the loss of only four aircraft. The operation as a whole was accordingly assessed as very successful.

Monday 24 July

Sergeant Geater and the rest of Flying Officer Merideth's crew returned from ten days' leave and were informed by their Flight Commander, Squadron Leader A.L. Williams, that PB 248 E for Easy was to be their own aircraft. This, they acknowledged as a happy arrangement; but not so Flight Lieutenant Stewart who had flown the aircraft on three previous operations and thought it should have been allocated to his crew.

There is something of a mystery concerning the reason that Flight Lieutenant Lines and his crew did not get their usual leave since it was normal practice for crews to fly three, possibly four operations, and then get ten days leave; as did Flying Officer Merideth's crew, who after the standard three trips went on leave from 14 July to 23 July. Merideth's crew had joined the squadron in mid-June and after returning from leave were just about to fly their fourth operation. A clear disparity in the allocation of operational duties is evident when one considers that Flight Lieutenant Lines' crew joined the squadron almost a month later (6 July), had already carried out four operations and were about to perform their fifth. By 24 July the crew were well overdue for some leave.

50

Operation 5: 24/25 July Donges

In the evening 18 crews were assigned for the night's operations: 9 were to fly to Donges to bomb oil storage tanks and a further 9 were to attack Stuttgart. A total of 104 Lancasters and 9 Mosquitos drawn from 5 and 8 Groups were to attack Donges and Flight Lieutenant Lines and crew were sent as part of this force. PB 304 was airborne at 2225 hours carrying a 13,000 lbs bomb load and 1,450 gallons of fuel. The route to France was via Bridport to 4920N 0300W and the time over target was between 0140 and 0150 hours.

106 SQUADRON ORDER OF BATTLE
Operation 5: 24/25 July Donges

Battle Order	Captain	A/C Serial No	ID Letter
1.	F/O Merideth	PB 248	E
2.	F/Lt Williams A G	PB 232	N
3.	F/Sgt Netherwood	PB 145	L
4.	F/Lt Lines	PB 304	S
5.	F/O Sayeau	PD 214	D
6.	F/Lt Jones	LM 215	F
7.	F/O Boivin	ND 331	G
8.	F/Lt Parry	PB 303	R
9.	F/O Paterson	LM 211	Z

Only four enemy aircraft were seen over the target area but search-lights were coning the bombers effectively up to 10,000 ft, and Wing Commander Woodroffe, the Master Bomber, was held in the lights for four minutes. Flying Officer Merideth's crew witnessed one Lancaster shot down from 9,000 ft with its port engines on fire and the aircraft was seen to hit the ground. Three Lancasters were lost at Donges, augmented by another 17 on the Stuttgart raid, as well as four Halifaxes. All aircraft were instructed to bomb on a track of 130 degrees true and the aiming point was marked with red and green Target Indicators. PB 304 bombed at 0143 hours from 10,500 ft and Bomber Command reports claim the target was devastated. PB 304 landed at 0336 hours.

All 106 Squadron aircraft returned safely, although for one of Flying Officer Merideth's crew, there was some very bad news at the end of the night. Flying Officer Neal, the navigator in Don Merideth's crew, lost his brother, who also happened to be a navigator on 50 Squadron based at Skellingthorpe. The two crews had gone through training together and had become very good friends. Their Lancaster LL 842, piloted by a Flying Officer Parker, was hit by flak near Nogent le Rotrou, 80 miles west of Paris and the aircraft burst into flames then exploded. Only Sergeant Hampton, the mid-upper gunner, managed to bale out just before the Lancaster blew up. Three of the crew were Canadians: Flying Officer Parker, Flying Officer Neal and Flight Sergeant Campbell.

Operation 6: 25 July St Cyr Air Park

Air Commodore Sharp, the 54 Base Commander visited the station together with Flight Lieutenant Belcher, an appropriately named catering officer, who after inspecting the kitchens and dining rooms reported that they were clean, well kept and the food attractive in appearance. Accompanying him on his inspection was Flight Lieutenant Feugard, the base catering officer, and they claimed that the diet and standards of cooking were satisfactory. Meanwhile 106 Squadron aircrew, most of whom had not gone to bed until after 6 o'clock, were woken up at noon and instructed to attend briefing at 1600 hours for operations that evening. They were also required to attend the flight offices as soon as possible.

Yet again 106 Squadron assigned more aircraft than any other unit and dispatched 20 Lancasters to St Cyr - the next highest contributor being 61 Squadron, which sent 18 aircraft. These formed part of a total of 104 aircraft from 5 Group, including 6 Mosquitos, to bomb an airfield and signals centre near Paris. PB 304 carried a 9,000 lbs bomb load (10 x 500 lb + 1 x 4,000 lb) and took-off at 1745 hours, the route out being via Reading - 5030N 0010W - target.

106 SQUADRON ORDER OF BATTLE
Operation 6: 25 July St Cyr Air Park

Battle Order	Captain	A/C Serial No	ID Letter
1.	S/Ldr Williams A L	PB 298	B
2.	F/O Durrant	JB 663	A
3.	F/O Browne	LL 953	C
4.	F/O Sayeau	PD 214	D
5.	F/O Merideth	PB 248	E
6.	F/Lt Jones	LM 215	F
7.	F/O Boivin	ND 331	G
8.	F/Lt Taylor	PB 191	H
9.	F/Sgt Netherwood	PB 145	L
10.	F/O Mavaut	PB 203	M
11.	F/O Fyson	PB 281	J

Battle Order	Captain	A/C Serial No	ID Letter
12.	F/O Pemberton	ME 778	O
13.	F/O Harris	LM 641	P
14.	F/Lt Lines	PB 304	S
15.	F/Lt Parry	PB 303	R
16.	F/O Thompson C E	JB 593	T
17.	F/O Thompson J G	PB 284	U
18.	S/Ldr Grindon	PB 296	X
19.	W/O Cunningham	ND 868	Q
20.	F/O Paterson	LM 211	Z

The time over the target was 1956 hours to 2000 hours and Flying Officer Steel released PB 304's bombs at 1956 hours from a height of 10,500 ft when they were seen to explode across the target. Overall the bombing was noted as being accurate and concentrated in spite of moderate to intense ground defence fire which resulted in a total of 49 aircraft being damaged by flak. Flying Officer Fyson's aircraft, PB 281, was caught in the searchlights and damaged to the extent of its starboard inner engine being put out of action. Another aircraft was hit by a fighter and two others damaged by a collision. All returned safely to England except LM 589 of 463 Squadron, flown by Flying Officer Grundy, which was hit by heavy flak and crashed. Four or five of the crew were seen to bale out, but some airmen, including those in Flying Officer Merideth's crew, witnessed light flak being fired at their parachutes. Defensive cover was provided by Spitfires of 11 Group, though this did not stop the Germans trying to get at the bombers as instanced by an Me 109 which opened fire on a Lancaster from 600 yards to port and beneath it. The front and mid-upper gunners returned the fire to such effect that the fighter crashed to the ground.

As it passed over the French coast PB 304 was fired on and hit by flak, probably from a coastal battery. The Lancaster was damaged in the tail and Sergeant Saul wounded in his right leg and left shoulder but there is no clear indication that the rear gunner's injuries were immediately life threatening, since Flight Lieutenant Lines continued onto Metheringham. The aircraft should have crossed the English coast at position 5030N 0010W, near The Isle of Wight, and had there been the need, he almost certainly would have diverted to the nearest airfield. PB 304 landed safely at 2145 hours and Sergeant Saul was taken to hospital, where he remained for the next ten days.

A remarkable and potentially disastrous incident occurred on this

operation when Flying Officer Ruff, the bomb aimer in Flying Officer
Harris' crew, reported that he had seen a bomb from his aircraft hit
another Lancaster below them. He said that it hit and bounced off the
rear turret, but that despite any damage the aircraft must undoubtedly have suffered, it continued on its course in normal fashion. Ruff's
bombs were released at 1957 hours from 12,000 ft and there is no
recorded information as to the identity of the other Lancaster,
although many other aircraft were below them including Flying Officer
Merideth's aircraft PB 248. Its bombs were also released at 1957 hours
from only 9,000 ft and the majority of 106 Squadron bombed from
below 12,000 ft. Nobody else reported the incident.

Operation 7: 26/27 July Givors

During the day there was a bit of a flap on and for a while rumours
of a daylight operation to be put on at short notice circulated around
the base. By late afternoon it was known that operations were on,
though bad weather was affecting Britain and France and many were
sure it would be called off. However it was not cancelled and at briefing the airmen learned that 106 Squadron was sending 19 Lancasters
to make up a force of 178, attacking the railway centre at Givors near
Lyons.

Because of Sergeant Saul's recent injuries he was unable to fly and it
is at this point that Sergeant Mohand Singh joined the crew of PB 304
to take over the rear turret. Although he had been with 106 Squadron
since December 1943, Singh had not flown on operations since the
night of 5/6 June. This was his twentieth trip and he had gained valuable experience that would have been welcomed in any crew. Despite
flak damage to its rear turret and tail on the St Cyr raid PB 304 was
made fit to fly and again allocated to Flight Lieutenant Lines.

106 SQUADRON ORDER OF BATTLE
Operation 7: 26/27 July Givors

Battle Order	Captain	A/C Serial No	ID Letter
1.	S/Ldr Williams A L	PB 298	B
2.	F/O Durrant	JB 663	A
3.	F/O Browne	LL 953	C
4.	F/O Sayeau	PD 214	D
5.	F/O Merideth	PB 248	E
6.	F/Lt Jones	LM 215	F
7.	F/O Boivin	ND 331	G
8.	F/Lt Taylor	PB 191	H

Battle Order	Captain	A/C Serial No	ID Letter
9.	F/Sgt Netherwood	PB 145	L
10.	F/O Mavaut	PB 203	M
11.	F/O Fyson	PB 281	J
12.	F/O Harris	LM 641	P
13.	F/Lt Lines	PB 304	S
14.	F/Lt Parry	PB 303	R
15.	F/O Thompson C E	JB 593	T
16.	F/O Thompson J G	PB 284	U
17.	S/Ldr Grindon	LM 211	Z
18.	F/O Archer	PB 296	X
19.	F/Lt Williams A G	PB 232	N

The weather forecast supplied to Air Staff at 1720 hours mentioned the threat of thunderstorms over the target area in the afternoon and evening, continuing into the night. Broken cloud was predicted over Givors below 10,000 ft, and had crews been aware of the conditions they were about to encounter, they would probably have been quite concerned.

When the Lancasters took-off from Metheringham it was raining hard and this was a taste of things to come throughout the night. PB 248 was the first aircraft off at 2120 hours and PB 304 followed at 2125 hours, each of the 106 Squadron aircraft being loaded with 9,000 lbs (7 x 1,000 lb + 4 x 500 lb). As the bombers flew south towards Bridport, the rain turned into heavy thunderstorms and wireless operators sat by their sets, anxiously awaiting a recall, should it be transmitted. Had one been sent out, it would have been difficult to understand anyway because the airwaves were full of static and other interference, making any message hard to interpret.

Flight Lieutenant Taylor arrived over the target at 0135 hours and found 10/10ths cloud that stretched down to ground level, with very bad visibility. He circled the target for half an hour and failed to see any markers, so set course for home, jettisoning his bombs on the way. Heavy rain lashed the aircrafts' windscreens as the Lancasters were buffeted up and down in a violent thunderstorm, so it is understandable that to avoid colliding with other aircraft, the majority of pilots chose to switch their navigation lights on and risk being spotted by a fighter. The lightning was blinding and the cloud seemed to stretch forever upwards, indeed Sergeant Geater intercepted a message between two Mosquito pilots, of whom one was telling the other, he had climbed to

22,000 ft and still remained in cloud.

The time over the target was supposed to be from 0207 hours to 0225 hours, but there was a delay marking the target caused by the weather, and many aircraft circled for at least twenty minutes. PB 304 bombed from 5,000 ft at 0214 hours, aiming at two green Target Indicators visible through the murk, and Flight Lieutenant Lines was one of only three captains to return with an aiming point photo. Altogether six aircraft were lost including two Mosquitos: two Lancasters due to collision and a Mosquito force landed - because it ran out of fuel. Flying Officer Gribbin's Mosquito, DZ 534, had its compass and Gee navigation equipment knocked out, before its air speed indicator became unserviceable and its fuel rapidly dwindled. At 0415 hours he transmitted an SOS which was answered by Exeter, the Mosquito finally ditching some 12 miles east of Cherbourg and the crew picked up by a US Navy vessel. The airmen had slight cuts and bruises but were otherwise unharmed by their experience.

PB 304 landed safely at 0620 hours and no doubt the crew were exhausted, having been airborne for eight hours and fifty five minutes. Flying Officer Durrant and his crew would certainly have been extremely happy to have survived the night and land at 0600 hours. This had been the last raid to complete their tour with 34 and 2/3rds operations behind them - the 2/3rds being two raids on French targets when each counted for only 1/3rd in April 1944. When the aircraft touched down at Metheringham, the weather had changed again and the crews returned to a pleasant, bright summer morning. This was not to last however.

Operation 8: 28/29 July Stuttgart

After a 24 hour break from flying at least some of the squadron personnel were feeling a little refreshed; the outcome of plenty of drink followed by much needed sleep. For some however the day began earlier than for others, when Flying Officer Merideth's crew were told to fly over to Woodbridge with Flying Officer Mavaut and some of his crew, who were to ferry ND 682 back to Metheringham. The Lancaster had been sitting at Woodbridge since the early hours of 5 July when it had been badly shot up and Mavaut's mid-upper gunner killed. During their return flight to Metheringham Sergeant Geater persuaded Flight Lieutenant Merideth to "beat up" his home town of Gillingham, on the River Medway, but forgot to mention it was designated a restricted military area. Someone reported them for low flying and back at base both pilot and wireless operator subsequently got into

1. Flight Lieutenant Peter Lines, former flying instructor at 15 Advanced Flying Unit and Pilot of Lancaster S for Sugar.

2. Sergeant Raymond Barnes
(Flight Engineer).

3. Flying Officer Harry Reid
(Navigator).

4. Flying Officer John Harvey-
Steel (Bomb Aimer).

5. Sergeant John Davenport
(Mid-upper Gunner).

trouble. The news that operations were definitely on did not cheer them up either - because a dance was being held in the NAAFI in aid of POW funds and everyone wanted to be there.

106 SQUADRON ORDER OF BATTLE

Operation 8: 28/29 July Stuttgart

Battle Order	Captain	A/C Serial No	ID Letter
1.	F/Lt Jones	JB 663	A
2.	F/O Kitto	LM 215	F
3.	F/O Browne	LL 953	C
4.	F/O Sayeau	PD 214	D
5.	F/O Merideth	PB 248	E
6.	F/Lt Williams A G	PB 232	N
7.	F/O Boivin	PB 298	B
8.	F/O Pemberton	ME 778	O
9.	F/Sgt Netherwood	PB 145	L
10.	F/O Mavaut	PB 203	M
11.	F/O Fyson	LM 641	P
12.	W/O Cunningham	ND 868	Q
13.	F/O Harris	LL 948	V
14.	F/Lt Lines	JB 593	T
15.	F/Lt Parry	PB 281	J
16.	F/O Archer	PB 296	X
17.	F/O Thompson J G	PB 284	U
18.	F/O Kipfer	LM 211	Z

5 GROUP ORDER OF BATTLE

9 Squadron	14 Lancasters
44 Squadron	14 Lancasters
49 Squadron	12 Lancasters
57 Squadron	15 Lancasters
61 Squadron	16 Lancasters
106 Squadron	18 Lancasters
619 Squadron	13 Lancasters
630 Squadron	12 Lancasters

It will be noticed that on this occasion Flight Lieutenant Lines and his crew were allocated JB 593, rather than their regular PB 304, which they had flown since their second operation. Having been delivered to the squadron in 1943, JB 593 was the only surviving Lancaster to have flown from its former base at Syerston and had taken part in the first raid from Metheringham on 18 November, 1943. Sergeant Singh knew it well. Flight Lieutenant Parry also changed aircraft, leaving PB 303 behind with its sister aircraft, possibly for some routine maintenance or repairs. The 18 Lancasters of 106 Squadron were part of a force of 494 aircraft from 1,3 5, and 8 Groups, and as is confirmed by the Order of Battle, 106 Squadron again contributed the highest number of aircraft.

JB 593 was airborne at 2205 hours carrying 12 "J" type cluster bombs and a single 2,000 pounder. Each of the 12 carriers contained fourteen 30 lb incendiary jet devices which, as they dropped, were designed to break up whilst falling through the air, scattering the small bombs as they fell to earth. It is claimed this weapon was unreliable and many failed to go off.

The route to Germany was via Reading to position 4948N 0030E: 4820N 0120E: 4813N 0350E: 4850N 0600E: 4900N 0730E: 4845N 0820E: Stuttgart. Times over the target were 0135 hours to 0157 hours and bomb aimers were given an order of preference to choose their aiming points with respect to the following priorities: (A) centre of mixed red and green TIs (B) centre of green TIs (C) centre of red TIs (D) centre of Wanganui flares, on a heading of 112 magnetic with bombsights set for true height. Flying Officer Steel observed both red and green Target Indicators and opted to bomb on the green ones, releasing them at 0153 hours from a height of 17,000 ft.

All 106 Squadron aircraft except one, chose to adopt a similar tactic and bombed onto green TIs, while the dissenter aimed at a Wanganui flare on a parachute. One cluster on Flight Sergeant Netherwood's aircraft, PB 145, hung up and was later jettisoned at 0239 hours. Fighter activity on the night was intense and Flying Officer Pemberton and his crew, in ME 778 were shot down at 0155 hours near Durmersheim. The young Australian pilot who had commenced operational flying with 106 Squadron on the night of 22/23 May died with all his crew and the seven airmen were buried at Bad Tolz Durnbach. Flying Officer Browne's Lancaster, LL 953, was also attacked by two nightfighters as it approached the target area and although the aircraft sustained severe damage, he just managed to make it back to base.

Because of extensive night-fighter activity there was very little flak thrown up at the bombers and the majority of the 39 Lancasters lost on the Stuttgart raid were accounted for by fighters. There were other operations this night at Forêt De Nieppe and Hamburg, when altogether 61 aircraft were lost. The Luftwaffe did not get its own way entirely however and a record number of fighters were destroyed.

Twenty seven of the enemy were confirmed as destroyed; six probably destroyed; with twelve damaged. These figures include sixteen Ju 88s, one Me 110 and one Me 410. Approximately 300 fighters were airborne on the night and about 200 of them attacked bombers heading for Stuttgart, where they were first intercepted near Orleans. A bright half moon helped the night-fighter crews to find their victims and they pursued the bombers into the early hours of the morning during the return leg.

When Flying Officer Browne arrived over the airfield, his Lancaster LL 953, was in a dangerous condition and hardly airworthy. He made a bumpy landing but then swung off the runway with the inevitable outcome that the aircraft had to be taken off strength for repair at a maintenance unit and did not fly again for several weeks. Flight Lieutenant Lines and his crew landed at 0530 hours after yet another long flight lasting seven hours and twenty five minutes.

Operation 9: 30 July Cahagnes - Normandy

On Saturday 29 July, the squadron was stood down but crews were warned to stand-by for operations early the following morning. Although it was summer the weather remained wet and overcast and it had been raining for nearly two full days. An air of gloom hung over Metheringham and heavy rain-bearing cloud made the fenlands of Lincolnshire quite depressing. Under such dismal conditions it was difficult for the crews to get out and enjoy themselves in the immediate vicinity and alternative activities were restricted because of the airfield's isolated position.

There were several sergeants' and officers' messes with bars on the camp but many airmen preferred the delights of Lincoln, where crews drank at The Saracen's Head. Those who worked hard, played hard, since as was readily conceded, the next opportunity for a few would be in the "next world" and most of those concerned with operations understood this, with very few feeling any resentment about their chances of survival. Airmen who drank locally went to The Red Lion or The Royal Oak in Martin, others to The Penny Farthing in Timberlands, which happened to be near the WAAF quarters and so became a particularly popular venue with those courting the girls in blue serge.

The early morning call on 30 July was at 0300 hours, for briefing at 0400. Some airmen had had a very late night, a few having only recently gone to bed, when they were called to get up again, whilst it was still raining and in no way different from the previous day Saturday. Some individuals went to the mess for breakfast, but many could not face food at that time of the morning. "For myself," former Sergeant Syd Geater recalled, "it was just a couple of cups of tea and then with Bruce (rear gunner) and Ron (flight engineer), we made our way to the briefing room. There we met up with the rest of our crew. The first and last thing we were told was that we had to take the utmost care today because our own troops were involved and if we had any doubts, then crews should return with their bombs." The Lancasters were to bomb six aiming points in Normandy around German positions, prior to another offensive by the British Second Army. The airstrike would be code-named, OPERATION BLUECOAT.

It was a dismal scene at Metheringham with tired airmen trudging around in the wet and dark; firstly to the mess, then briefing, then the flight locker room where personal possessions were left behind and finally to the parachute store for transport out to the waiting aircraft. Flight Lieutenant Lines and his crew were number thirteen on the Order of Battle and rostered to fly in their usual aircraft, PB 304. The dispersal point for S for Sugar was near Barff Farm, close to the north-western end of the 4,200 ft runway 13 (No 6). Across the taxiway sat its sister aircraft PB 303 R for Robert, parked next to it was PB 284 U for Uncle, and next to that LM 641 P for Peter.

After reaching the aircraft, checks were carried out to clear any last minute snags and Sergeant Barnes together with his pilot inspected external panels and ensured that all control locks, together with the Pitot-head cover, had been removed. Any serious oil drips were investigated and tyres checked for wear and to ensure that there was no creep on the wheels. Flying Officer Steel made sure the eighteen 500 lb bombs comprising the bomb load were secure and that the circuitry was correct, each having been fitted with a type 44 pistol and the distributor set for a stick spacing of 20 yards. The two gunners checked their turrets were free and able to rotate without restriction and that the gun workings moved easily and breeches were clear from obstructions. As Flying Officer Reid checked his charts and made last minute calculations, Sergeant Young warmed up the TR1154/1155 radio but was not permitted to carry out any checks as complete radio silence had to be maintained. German operator's were constantly monitoring all radio traffic and any breach of silence would warn them that operations were on. With all the formalities completed the engines were started and further checks made on the flaps and flying controls. Once everything proved to be in working order Flight Lieutenant Lines could at last sign the Form 700, the flight authorization and his formal acceptance of the aeroplane.

At 0500 hours, the cloud base was down to 500 ft and although a slight breeze arose from the north-east, getting up to 15 knots by 1000 hours, it was not enough to blow away the murk. With under an hour to take-off time the engines were shut down again and the crew got out of the aircraft, for a final cigarette and chat with the ground crew. Then, from the control tower balcony in the distance a green Very light was fired and the men climbed back into the bombers and the doors slammed shut for the last time. One by one the Lancasters made their way along the taxiway to the threshold of the active runway, which on this particular morning was runway 02 (No 4) because of a 10 knot wind blowing from the north-east.

In the ORB it states that PB 304 took-off at 0555 hours but the same time is recorded for a number of aircraft and Wing Commander Piercy's gunner, Sergeant Stan Goodman, noted that his aircraft took-off at 0605 and they were number 1 on the Order of Battle. When their turn came a controller in the runway caravan flashed a green Aldis lamp and the throttles were pushed forward, Sergeant Barnes following his pilot through with the palm of his hand, holding the throttle levers firm against the gate. Once they were airborne Barnes raised the undercarriage, while Flight Lieutenant Lines at a safe height adjusted the power settings and PB 304 joined those Lancasters from 106 Squadron, climbing steadily eastwards towards Coningsby. The bombers climbed into the air at thirty second intervals, so it took over ten minutes to get them all airborne and on reaching overhead Coningsby the 106 Squadron Lancasters joined two formations of three aircraft from 83 Squadron, as part of "Red Force".

OPERATION BLUECOAT was the fourth in a series of army support operations which began on the night of 14/15 June, 1944, and 106 Squadron dispatched a total of 21 Lancasters within a force of 692 bombers from 1, 3, 4, 5, 6, and 8 Groups, which broke down to 462 Lancasters, 200 Halifaxes and 30 Mosquitos. There was one early return. Originally 5 Group intended sending 207 Lancasters on this operation but in the end it managed only 184 and the numbers from the other groups were also reduced probably because of a combination of bad weather and the heavy losses sustained on the night of 28 July. The six different aiming points were contained in a triangular area to the south-east of Caumont flanked by the towns of Villers Bocage, Jurques, and Cahagnes. Aiming point "C" was the 106 Squadron target which lay only 6,000 yards away from the positions of XXX Corps, near Cahagnes. Wing Commander Piercy led the force from 106 Squadron in ND 682 K for King, the Lancaster on its first operational flight since 4 July.

106 SQUADRON ORDER OF BATTLE
Operation 9: BLUECOAT: 30 July Cahagnes - Normandy

Battle Order	Captain	A/C Serial No	ID Letter
1.	W/Cdr Piercy	ND 682	K
2.	F/Lt Jones	JB 663	A
3.	S/Ldr Williams A L	PB 298	B
4.	F/O Sayeau	PD 214	D
5.	F/O Merideth	PB 248	E
6.	F/O Kitto	LM 215	F
7.	F/Lt Taylor	PB 191	H
8.	F/Sgt Netherwood	PB 145	L
9.	F/O Boivin	PB 281	J
10.	F/O Mavaut	PB 203	M
11.	S/Ldr Grindon	JB 593	T
12.	F/Lt Parry	PB 303	R
13.	F/Lt Lines	PB 304	S
14.	F/O Thompson J G	PB 284	U
15.	F/O Harris	LL 948	V
16.	F/O Kipfer	LM 211	Z
17.	W/Off Cunningham	ND 868	Q
18.	F/O Archer	PB 296	X
19.	F/O Fyson	LM 641	P
20.	F/Lt Williams A G	PB 232	N
21.	F/O Browne	ND 331	G

5 GROUP ORDER OF BATTLE

9 Squadron	14 Lancasters
44 Squadron	12 Lancasters
49 Squadron	12 Lancasters
50 Squadron	14 Lancasters
57 Squadron	13 Lancasters
61 Squadron	15 Lancasters
83 Squadron	6 Lancasters
97 Squadron	6 Lancasters
106 Squadron	21 Lancasters
207 Squadron	14 Lancasters
463 Squadron	15 Lancasters
467 Squadron	15 Lancasters
619 Squadron	14 Lancasters
627 Squadron	1 Mosquito
630 Squadron	12 Lancasters

Six Lancasters from 97 Squadron set course for Waddington and they were to lead "Green Force" and attack Aiming Point "D". The combined force was to cruise towards the south coast at 155 mph, climbing to 6,000 ft and routing via Woodley near Reading to positions 5130N 0050W 5047N 0040W 5000N 0050W - Target. As the bombers crossed the English coast, Very cartridges, a red one from Red Force and a green from Green Force, were to be fired from the leading aircraft, signalling that speed was to be increased to 180 mph.

The weather, which was about to play a big part in the day's events, showed little sign of improvement as the bombers headed south towards Normandy. The route forecast supplied to the Air Staff at 0430 hours that morning, predicted 9/10ths cloud in two layers, with the lowest between 5 - 6,000 ft and the upper at 7 -10,000 ft. Wind was forecast as 26 miles per hour at 7,000 feet and, 20 mph at 2,000 ft, its strength and direction being a major factor on all bombing raids and accurate reporting of it vital to the navigator and bomb aimer. Every half hour the wireless operator would listen out for the weather bulletins, and with a possible recall signal due Sergeant Young listened to all the signals traffic for any urgent messages.

Flying in loose formation towards the English Channel the force from Bomber Command grew larger as it passed above Reading, the confluence of the tracks taken by aircraft of different groups. Just crossing the English coast the bombers emerged into brilliant sunshine, but on the flight decks airmen could see ahead of them bad weather and a concentration of huge cumulo- nimbus cloud in front of them. An area of low pressure was centred on the Wash and a cold front moving slowly north-easterly up the Channel had plenty of cloud and rain in it, a feature which was to influence the day's events.

Chapter 5

THE BATTLE IN THE CLOUDS

When Bomber Command commenced daylight operations after D-Day Lancasters in 5 Group were painted with markings and insignia to enable the aircraft of the officers leading an operation to be more easily identified. 106 Squadron had begun changing over to daylight colours at the end of June when tail-fins were painted white and some with green stripes. On 30 July the Lancasters flown by section leaders of 83 Squadron had one foot wide vertical stripes on their fins. The leading aircraft from 97 Squadron displayed white letters, with two horizontal white stripes on the outside of each fin. The crews carried Aldis lamps on board and each base was allocated a colour of the day, to provide a visual signals back-up, should it be required.

On a day when the weather was as bad as 30 July visual recognition of the target was much more important than identifying who was who in the air - but it could only be done by flying beneath the cloud when it had been planned to bomb from heights of between 6,000 to 10,000 ft. With troops of the British 2nd Army only a short distance away and the cloud base as low as 2,000 ft normal procedures had to be abandoned and the chances of delivering an accurate attack above that height seemed very remote. Things got off to a bad start and at 0730 hours the crews in the Halifaxes of 4 Group abandoned any hope of attacking Aiming Point "G" and eventually aborted the raid.

Some of the first aircraft into action this Sunday morning were however Halifaxes, those from 6 Group squadrons with mainly Canadian crews and 420 Snowy Owl Squadron had taken-off from its base at Tholthorpe at 0543. Their target was Aiming Point "B" at Amye-Sur-Suellees, a small village approximately a mile-and-a-half east of Cahagnes. The Halifax mark IIIs with their Bristol Hercules engines carried 16 x 500 lbs of general purpose bombs. Pilot Officer Johnstone in B for Baker, led the attack and dropped his at 0748 and whilst conditions may have varied over short distances, the low cloud was nevertheless breaking up to good effect at this time. Wing Commander McKenna bombed onto yellow Target Indicators at 0751 from 3,000 ft and his comments were that he had made a good hit as long as the target had been correctly marked.

ALLOCATED BOMBING TIMES AND AIMING POINTS

Group	Bombing Times	Aiming Points	Position	
4 Group	0730 to 0735	G	4904N	0041W
6 Group	0745 to 0755	B	4904N	0043W
3 Group	0745 to 0755	B	4904N	0043W
5 Group	0800 to 0803	C	4903N	0044W
5 Group	0800 to 0803	D	4902N	0047W
1 Group	0815 to 0820	E	4902N	0046W
8 Group	0815 to 0820	E	4902N	0046W
1 Group	0830 to 0835	F	4903N	0046W

The 8 Group Lancasters of the Pathfinder Force, responsible for backing up the initial marking laid down by the "Oboe" Mosquitos, ran into difficulties early on when 156 Squadron from Warboys was only approaching the target, as some crews were already being ordered to abort. Squadron Leader Ison, checked with Wing Commander Broadhurst the Master Bomber at 0800 hours, and was ordered to descend to the "basement" at 3,000 ft. The Master Bomber had been instructed not to attack four of the aiming points below that height, for fear of the bombers being hit by anti-aircraft fire. From 3,000 ft the ground remained obscured by thick cloud and 156 Squadron were left to orbit the battlefield along with several other squadrons.

Amongst other squadrons responsible for illuminating the aiming points were 13 Lancasters from 35 Squadron at Gravely and Flight Lieutenant Gooch, pilot of PB 288 P for Peter, complained that broadcasts from the Master Bomber were being drowned out by someone calling, "A for Apple - B for Beer - C for Charlie", in quick succession. Flying Officer Marsden flying PB 259 C for Charlie claimed that the Master Bomber's voice could hardly be heard and poor communication was a major feature of this operation when many crews failed to understand R/T and W/T messages.

106 Squadron was not called down to bomb by the Master Bomber and PB 304 along with the other 20 Lancasters circled the battlefield awaiting orders. As they and other heavy bombers arrived on the scene the desperation of the situation was observed by Wing Commander Curry from his Mosquito, KB 195. Below his aircraft he noted that some Lancasters were flying through cloud with their wheels down and that others were flying as low as 800 ft. These sightings occurred between 0758 and 0803, as the Wing Commander swooped above the main bombing stream taking photographs at 1,000 ft and it seems that some squadrons in 3 Group used this unusual practice to slow the air-

craft down and to descend more quickly. 106 Squadron Lancasters were above the target area between approximately 0745 and 0808 hours.

Some squadrons in 5 Group were called down to attack the objectives but by 0800 hours the majority of crews had abandoned any real hope of seeing the TIs or the aiming points. The target for 50 Squadron was also Cahagnes and its 14 Lancasters were airborne from Skellingthorpe at 0555. All but one aircraft returned with the bomb loads, after abandoning the operation on instructions from the Master Bomber. The exception was Flying Officer Harspool's aircraft, whose crew attacked the primary target at 0809 hours from 2,000 ft. He reported that his bombs fell onto smoke, rising from a Target Indicator and hit some buildings but it is not known whether Flying Officer Harspool acted on his own initiative or was ordered in to attack by the Master Bomber.

Aiming Point "D" situated to the south of Cahagnes and southeast of Aiming Point "C", came under attack from the Lancasters of 97 Straits Settlement Squadron led by its Commanding Officer, Wing Commander Heward. On a normal operation the crews of 97 Squadron along with those of 83, which was also based at Coningsby, would have marked and illuminated the aiming points, as part of the 5 Group marker force. The Air Officer Commanding 5 Group, Air Vice-Marshal Cochrane had created, what has often been referred to as his "Independent Air Force", which frequently operated separately from the main force and used a different method to mark aiming points than Air Vice-Marshal Bennett's 8 Group Pathfinders.

Rather than use the radio guided system of Oboe, Mosquitos of 627 Squadron operating from Woodhall Spa were used to fly in very low, often below 500 ft and visually identify the aiming points. These were then marked with red spot flares, so that the Lancasters of 83 and 97 Squadrons could further illuminate the target, prior to the arrival of the main force. On 30 July however both 83 and 97 were part of the main force and had no special role or function. The six Lancasters of 97 Squadron had taken-off from Coningsby at 0540 hours and their crews' objective was aiming point "D". Wing Commander Heward led a formation of three aircraft in PA 974 B for Baker, supported by his wingmen, Flight Lieutenant Baker in NE 121 and Flight Lieutenant Bucknell in ND 840.

Heward identified the target visually by a red Oboe marker and noted the cloud ceiling to be 4,000 ft but five minutes before he attacked, the Master Bomber broadcast to the main force that the ceiling was now 2,000 ft. He descended to that height and on running in towards the aiming point he observed smoke rising from a burned out Target Indicator, and on his port side slightly behind him, another red Target Indicator going down. This second marker was slightly ahead of the others which were concentrated, and he therefore judged the latter position to be where he should aim his bombs. Just before they were released, the bomb aimer, Flight Lieutenant Pelden, saw a house on fire approximately one mile to starboard of track which might have been the building hit by the bombs from Flying Officer Harspool's aircraft only minutes before.

Most of the 97 Squadron Lancasters carried extra crew members and NE 121 had a second wireless operator on board and a visual bomb aimer, who was probably a flight engineer. For this nine man crew the descent was a perilous one which cost some their lives. Having spoken to his section leader on the VHF radio, Flight Lieutenant Baker flying NE 121, went down through the cloud and when his accompanying aircraft emerged beneath it, the crews noticed that his aircraft was missing. Tragically no further messages were received from Baker's aircraft.

None of the other crews from 97 Squadron attacked the target, though some did descend with the intention of doing so, prior to them receiving "Apple Pie", the code-word transmitted to signify that the operation had been aborted. Flight Lieutenant Bucknell broke cloud at 1,200 ft but overshot the target so that by the time he had gone around again the message to abort had been received. Flight Sergeant Woolnough in ND 501 T for Tommy, went down to 1,000 ft above the target area at 0800 hours, but still found it covered by cloud and at 0805 he acknowledged the signal to abort. Despite the bad weather there was no lack of enthusiasm and Squadron Leader Belleroche also made several runs at the target before abandoning the mission at 0806.

As the earlier arrivals were abandoning the operation those crews fresh on the scene continued to orbit and wait for improvements in the weather or new orders from the Master Bomber. This understandably caused some confusion and exacerbated the risks caused by frustration, noted by Squadron Leader Ison of 156 Squadron who was ordered down to 2,000 ft at 0814 hours. 156 Squadron Lancasters each carried 10 x 500 lb bombs and 8 yellow Target Indicators, types "A" and "B". By 0818 much smoke had risen from the ground which as it swirled into the air, mixed with the low cloud, to obscure the targets even further. Ison had already observed that of those aircraft being called down, some crews were beginning to undershoot the aiming point and he was worried in case bombs fell behind Allied lines. Up to this operation no

Allied troops had been killed by British bombs and no squadron wanted to be the first to make such an error. Many senior airmen privately feared such a disaster and knew it was only a matter of time before it happened. Flight Lieutenant Owens, who had followed Ison down, claimed one stick of bombs undershot by a mile and proved a definite danger to Allied forces, who may well have been relieved when the aircraft cleared the target altogether.

9 Squadron dispatched 14 Lancasters from Bardney but abandoned the operation at 0805 hours on receipt of the abort signal. Amongst their number was W4 964 J for "Johnny Walker" an old B1, which had already completed many missions but was due for a major overhaul. It later returned to squadron service and eventually completed no fewer than 106 operations to survive the war. Wing Commander Humphreys of 57 Squadron was above the target at 0800 hours, having abandoned the raid at 0758. The squadron's aiming point was to have been the same as that allocated to 106 Squadron and Wing Commander Humphreys later claimed that a precision attack had been impossible with the cloud base for the most part below 2,000 ft.

At least one veteran airman had a very cavalier approach to the way that the operation should have been organized. Group Captain Evans-Evans, the Station Commander at Coningsby, who had been flying in the RAF since 1924 was something of a character who regularly appeared at the end of the Coningsby runway, to wave to his crews as they took-off. On this occasion he was flying himself to keep his hand in, although his enthusiasm was not always appreciated by those who accompanied him. Group Captain Evans-Evans was not impressed by the way in which the Master Bomber handled the situation and in particular he failed, the group captain claimed, because he did not take the whole force down beneath the cloud. This prompted him to observe after the operation that he, "Obeyed orders to abort with extreme reluctance." For a senior officer to express such dissent was quite unusual and to some degree irresponsible. The Master Bomber being in charge of the whole force was infinitely more likely to have a better picture of what was happening and in any case be privy to information denied to others. The risks posed by 600 aircraft, many as low as 2,000 ft flying blind through cloud in such a confined area would have been unacceptable to most airmen.

Group Captain Evans-Evans had some support though and one of those who agreed with him was Wing Commander Deane the leader of Red Force and the six Lancasters from 83 Squadron. Flying in Lancaster ND 824, Deane estimated the cloud as a 10/10ths covering with tops at 5,000 ft and a base at around 3,500 ft. None of his crews spotted the Target Indicators before they heard the abort signal at 0759 hours – in spite of which Deane was also of the opinion that if the whole force had been taken down beneath the cloud, a successful attack could have been made.

For some crews things were going to plan when the raid was called off and they failed to understand the reasons for this instruction as instanced by Flight Lieutenant Kelly from 83 Squadron who was in a good position to bomb when he received the order to abort on High Frequency Channel "C". Most of the other pilots talked about messages being sent over the VHF radio and HF was normally used only for long distance communications, as between a ground station and aircraft in flight. 5 Group Headquarters did have a direct HF radio link but only with certain crews and it poses the question, as to who actually did give the order to abandon the operation?

While they circled the target area at a height of about 6,000 ft each crew member on board PB 304 scanned the sky keeping a sharp lookout for any other aircraft. They had already been up for nearly five hours and while feeling tired, they like other airmen accepted the needed for concentration, both to avoid flak and collision with other bombers. While Flight Lieutenant Lines was kept busy with the controls, Sergeant Barnes kept watch to starboard, as well as trying to monitor the dials on his panel. Flying Officer Steel would have been below in the bomb aimer's compartment keeping an eye out, while Flying Officer Reid observed activity on the port side of the Lancaster. Some wireless operators went up into the astrodome to see what was happening above and their leads stretched just enough to allow them to listen out for any vital messages. Just before 0800 hours Sergeant Young heard the abort signal and other transmissions soon followed, giving his pilot instructions for their course back to base.

Only a single Lancaster of 44 Squadron managed to push home an attack on Cahagnes when Flying Officer Brady dropped his 12 x 500 lb bombs on Aiming Point "D" from 1,200 ft but this was a lone strike since none of the other 11 Lancasters from 44 made a run. Amongst many of the crews of 5 Group, there was a lot of confusion about what should do done with the bomb loads and what route they should take for home. Additionally there was also a mix up over the use of some codewords and a difference of opinions in interpreting the correct signal that meant the operation had been aborted. On this occasion the two codewords used by 5 Group giving the order to abort, were "Apple Pie" and "Marmalade". 97 and 9 Squadron records, amongst others, refer to Apple Pie, while 83 Squadron acknowledged Marmalade.

What probably caused some confusion was that the Master Bomber used a codeword to cancel markers which were incorrectly placed and some crews mixed it up with the abort signal. At briefing that morning I have been told that some airmen only wrote down details on cigarette packets, while others used the back of their hands. It is hardly surprising that crews got things mixed up! Each group had its own codewords and 6 Group squadrons had been issued with "Lemon" to cancel and "Monkey Nuts", to abort. In the circumstances the latter just about summed up the day and everything that went wrong with this operation!

On checking his log book former Sergeant Geater found that he thought Marmalade to be the correct codeword and he received it at 0759 hours. He said that his pilot, Flying Officer Merideth heard the message before he did because it had been transmitted on the VHF radio a couple of minutes before the W/T message was received. The aircraft continued to orbit above the battlefield for a while until the route home was confirmed, when the crews waiting to attack Aiming Point "C" were instructed to carry out a wide left turn to position 4950N 0020W. They were then to proceed to other co-ordinates taking the bombers just inland of Portland Bill. Crews in 5 Group aircraft targeting Aiming Point "D" performed a wide right turn to position 5035N 0205W.

There were now an awful lot of aircraft circling or departing the airspace above Normandy heading in every direction at different heights, with even more American bombers on their way. Even the Station Commander from 158 Squadron's base at Lissett, Group Captain Sawyer whose Halifax had left the target area earlier than most admitted that it was frustrating and alarming to fly around in thick cloud, with the knowledge that there were another few hundred aircraft close by doing precisely the same thing. After receiving the abort signal he flew straight on for a while before climbing away and setting course for home.

Some groups had been more successful than others and certainly those from 1 Group, making their attacks a little later than the rest, did not have the same problems with the weather. 1 Group aircraft were above the target between 0815 to 0838 hours, during which time 103 Squadron from Elsham Wold contributed some nine Lancasters to the Bluecoat Operation - a number which would probably have been greater had it not suffered the loss of three aircraft two nights earlier on the Suttgart raid. The force from 103 was led by Squadron Leader

F.V.P. Van Rolleghem who observed that their markers were well placed and German ground defences light. All of 103 Squadron's aircraft carried 20 x 500lb instantaneously fused bombs, which they dropped on Aiming Point "F" at Forêt de Nieppe from 1,900 ft when they were above the target at 0830 hours - all nine Lancasters successfully completing the operation. Flight Lieutenant Furlong's aircraft was the last one to attack at 0842 and although the weather conditions encountered by 103 Squadron are not recorded, other factors suggest a gradual improvement took place with the cloud slowly lifting as the morning went on.

The claim by Squadron Leader Van Rolleghem that the German defences were light, was not the experience of the majority of crews in 3 Group, as instanced by Flight Sergeant Braun of 115 Squadron who reported that his aircraft was hit by machine-gun bullets. He made his bombing run at 1,000 ft but the bombs hung up until they were forced out by the jettison bar and another Lancaster from 1 Group was hit by flak in a position south-east of St Lô, resulting in its starboard fuel tank being badly holed. A German flak battery was sited near Amaye and it is claimed that this was later destroyed by a single Lancaster from 1 Group, which dropped 18 x 500 lb bombs upon it. The Germans were short of heavy artillery but had sufficient 20, 37, and 88 mm guns to put up an effective barrage and while the bombers were flying so low, light flak was just as bad as that thrown up by the heavier guns.

OPERATION BLUECOAT

Tonnage of bombs dropped, including Target Indicators during successful attacks on 30 July.

Group	No of Aircraft	Type	Tonnage	T.I.s	Total
1.	102	Lancaster	427	0	427
3.	99	Lancaster	389	0	389
4.	0	Halifax	0	0	0
5.	6	Lancaster	27	0	27
6.	97	Halifax	337	0	337
8.	21	Mosquito	0	9	9
	53	Lancaster	183	10	193
Grand Totals	378		1363	19	1382

As they headed home the crews of 5 Group squadrons were now left with two main problems: first of all a large number of Lancasters still had bombs on board. Crews had to return their aircraft and make safe landings at airfields in England reporting bad visibility and covered with low cloud. During the main briefing that morning it had been impressed upon all airmen, not just pilots, to return any bombs not used on the target and under no circumstances should they jettison them in the English Channel. These were critical days of support for the Allied forces in Normandy the logistics of supply demanded a heavy concentration of shipping in this small and crowded stretch of water. How seriously this order was regarded by some captains can be gathered from their actions.

Flying Officer Brady of 44 Squadron heard a radio message, instructing crews to "Lighten their all-up weights". The origin of the broadcast was unknown but it could clearly be interpreted in two ways - and might have been taken by pilots to either burn off fuel, or jettison their bomb loads - perhaps enigmatic authorization for what many pilots were planning to do anyway: drop their bombs into the sea. The aircraft would certainly have handled more easily without them and the prospects of survival in the event of a forced landing would have materially increased. Many skippers may have been reluctant to burn off or dump fuel because they did not know what lay ahead of them and with airfields in Lincolnshire and Yorkshire covered in low cloud every gallon of fuel might be required to divert or hold off until the weather improved.

Squadron Leader Hildred of 44 Squadron, reported seeing many aircraft jettisoning bombs while flying on track across the English Channel, visibility above the cloud being quite good and this activity easy to observe. Most pilots logged the time and position of where they released their bomb loads. There were many different kinds of vessels in the sea and the Royal Navy in particular had a notorious reputation for shooting at any aircraft which dared to fly above its ships. Several pilots reported their aircraft fired upon by the Navy, whose twitchy gunners after the Battle for Crete, resented even the threat that friendly forces posed for them.

Flying Officer Slade of 44 Squadron jettisoned his 12 x 500 lb bombs at 5022N 0035E from 7,500 ft at 0829 revealing his position at that time as approximately twenty-five miles south-east of Beachy Head. The 12 Halifaxes from 158 Squadron in 4 Group, jettisoned into the Channel and the North Sea. Despite 16 Target Indicators going down on Aiming Point "G", the illuminators from 35 Squadron had either been unsure of their position or unable to identify it. Warrant Officer Collins of 158 Squadron in N for Nuts had recently had a narrow escape when his aircraft had crashed on take-off and he clearly was not taking any chances, jettisoning his bombs off Flamborough Head at 5404N 0103E, from 5,000 ft at 0932 hours. It is interesting to note that several crews from 158 Squadron only abandoned part of their bomb loads, as testified by Flying Officer Christian who in C for Charlie released only 3 x 500 lb bombs and kept 13 on board. He had abandoned the operation at 0730 hours, along with the other 4 Group crews, a good twenty five minutes before 106 Squadron arrived in the area. Flight Lieutenant Salter, also of 158, dropped his bombs at an unconfirmed position near the French coast. The crews of 4 Group seem to have flown a variety of routes on the return leg and there were great differences in the period of time between their abandoning the raid and landing in England.

Due to misunderstandings and general communications problems, many pilots and wireless operators claimed they failed to receive the anticipated broadcast instructions concerning the routing back to bases in England. The majority of 44 Squadron crews picked up the messages satisfactorily and a number of them followed the correct instructions. Flying Officer Heath in D for Dog, heard the 5 Group routing as Pershore Hawarden (Chester) - Squires Gate (Blackpool) - Wash on H2s or Gee lattice line to base and this message was transmitted at 0820 hours. Pershore is approximately eight miles east of Worcester and fifteen south of Birmingham so that to follow this course the bombers would have flown a long and circuitous route, burning off fuel and passing time until the weather cleared. Squadron Leader Hildred who had earlier reported crews disobeying orders and jettisoning their bombs, routed via Pershore and followed the recommended course. Flying Officer Lewis went via Reading - Cambridge - Doncaster - Wainfleet, to base. Not all 44 Squadron crews agreed on what they heard and at least two failed to understand R/T messages.

Flying Officer Squibb or at least his wireless operator, misunderstood W/T signals and landed at Blackpool which famous northern resort had already witnessed much air activity during the war years. The Wellington bomber itself was built at Squires Gate, amongst other places, and the town's position on the west coast gave it relatively good protection. Airmen and airwomen "sparks" were trained at Blackpool's number 10 Signals Recruitment Centre and The Winter Gardens was one of several places in the town turned over to the RAF. On 17 April, 1942, Squadron Leader J.D. Nettleton landed his badly shot up Lancaster at Blackpool, on his return from Augsburg. 12 Lancasters were dispatched on the famous daylight raid, but only five got back. Nettleton was later awarded The Victoria Cross.

Flight Sergeant Woolnough of 97 Squadron also got it wrong when after abandoning the mission at 0805 his wireless operator, Sergeant

Smith, received a signal which was read as instructions to land at Pershore where he touched down at 0922. Another diversion message was later transmitted and a new route given as 5116N 0045W 5214N 004W - Wash to base on Gee lattice line. This second course would take the bombers south of Farnborough, overhead Slough, Bovingdon and Luton, across country to a point near Gravely, from where they were to head north towards the Wash and their bases in Lincolnshire.

Depending on what wireless operators had heard previously this probably only added to the overall confusion. As they listened in on their TR 1154/55 Transmitter/Receivers tuned to group frequencies a few wireless operators had heard different codewords from what they expected and at least two different versions of the advised return routing - transmitted in both Morse and Wireless Telegraphy. The equipment was not totally reliable anyway and the amount of signals traffic fairly heavy.

Bad communication was not a new phenomenon on Bomber Command operations and on the odd occasion it cost a lot of airmen their lives. During an attack on Mailly-Le-Camp on 3 May, 1944, the Main Force Controller, Wing Commander Deane, had his transmissions drowned-out by dance band music being broadcast from an American forces station. That caused a delay giving the Germans time to organize their defences with such effect that the Luftwaffe were able to arrive in force and 42 Lancasters were lost. Later on it was discovered that the wing commander's radio had been incorrectly tuned.

It is possible that the second diversion signal may have been sent out because a Duty Officer at Bomber Command Headquarters, realized the potential danger created by 600 aircraft returning to weather bound airfields in England at more or less the same time. The decision to split the force up made sense but in the end instructions could only really be advisory and some pilots and navigators chose to go their own way. The majority of pilots in 5 Group followed the original routing via Pershore. Others such as 103 Squadron in 1 Group, flew back via Bridport and Upper Heyford, while a few flew up the North Sea before tracking west and inland towards Woodbridge.

From the beginning the BLUECOAT air support was something of a shambles and under normal circumstances would have been cancelled. Bomber Command Headquarters had come under a certain amount of pressure to carry out the operation since in the early hours of Sunday 30 July, British Second Army HQ had sent a signal to High Wycombe requesting it dispatch as many aircraft as possible - because with or without the support of the RAF, the attack was going ahead as scheduled. Although the weather forecast supplied to the Air Staff at 0430 did not suggest conditions were good enough for the bombers to land safely on their return before 1100 hours, observing that the best conditions would be found in the area of the south coast and around Exeter in particular. The weather forecast supplied to Chiefs of Staff will be discussed in more detail in another chapter.

Despite the fact that a large part of the force aborted, Christopher Buckley of the *Daily Telegraph* and a well known war correspondent, claimed this air operation was one of the most astonishing bombing raids of the war. He reported that the RAF performed marvellously in conditions which would normally have been regarded as impossible and that until literally seconds before they bombed, the aircraft were still hidden in cloud, consequently as the bombers dived towards the ground they were met by only light flak and small arms fire. What Buckley failed to appreciate was the risks that the crews were taking.

Some Lancasters in 3 Group received structural damage caused by blast, because crews were flying them too low when they dropped their bombs. Fuses fitted to the bombs were in most cases instantaneous, or at the most inserted with $1/2$ second delay fuses. Those who took such risks were well aware of what they were doing and in some crews airmen had a self-interest in so far as they knew that below them, might be their brothers and friends fighting for their lives. It is to the credit of those pilots and crews ordered down by the Master Bomber that they unhesitatingly took their chances and accepted the increased risk of flak and blast damage which threatened their aircraft.

By 0830 hours the 21 Lancasters from 106 Squadron, together with other aircraft from 5 Group, were on their way back, crossing the English coast between Bridport and Torquay in Lyme Bay, before setting course for Pershore. Just about as they were heading for home, twin-engined Martin Marauders of the American 9th Air Force were approaching Normandy, to add to the already congested sky and bomb positions in front of VIII Corps. As might have been predictable they also encountered difficulties because of the low cloud and generally bad weather, forcing at least 60 of them to abort the operation.

The returning force of Lancasters climbed to heights of between 7,000 and 9,000 ft, cruising at 165 mph and after crossing the Channel Flight Lieutenant Lines followed the recommended routing towards Pershore before flying on an approximate north-westerly heading to pass overhead or abeam Hawarden on the outskirts of Chester. Not all 106 Squadron's Lancasters made it past Pershore and Flying Officer Kitto in LM 215 F for Freddy landed there by mistake at 0920; just two minutes before Flight Sergeant Woolnough's Lancaster. Kitto's wireless operator, Sergeant Whitaker, was another victim of the confused messages and both he and his pilot thought they were being ordered to land at Hawarden. No crew from 106 Squadron dumped their bombs but returned them to Metheringham as instructed.

By 0900 hours the cloud base at Metheringham was a 7/10ths covering at 800 ft and the picture was much the same across the country as a whole. Navigators were kept busy working out the various options, checking the weather with wireless operators and assessing conditions for possible diversion airfields whilst flight engineers monitored the fuel consumption to make fine calulations about the amount of burn off and what they should keep in reserve. They consulted their pilots and agreed on power settings, while the gunners maintained a lookout for any breaks in the cloud and landmarks beneath them. The flight deck crews would have been fully occupied with matters in hand and it is possible that on board PB 304 the earliest indications of trouble, in the form of an overheating engine or fuel flow went unnoticed.

From Hawarden PB 304 flew on to Squires Gate at Blackpool, where several aircraft had already landed by mistake and en route from Chester to Blackpool, the flight path would have taken the Lancaster close to the port of Liverpool, which was a heavily defended area to be avoided at all costs. Training flights from busy airfields at Cark, Millom and Walney Island flew down the west coast but most pilots were aware of the dangers from the port's anti-aircraft guns. Presumably Flying Officer Reid had charts to warn him of all danger areas and after safely reaching Blackpool the flight to Metheringham, a distance of approximately 130 miles on a south-easterly track, should have been completed with ease. The flight path would take the bomber north of Manchester, across the Pennine Hills and abeam of Sheffield where it was soon into familiar territory and the fenlands of Lincolnshire, with an abundance of airfields below them.

The first aircraft of 106 Squadron to touch down at Metheringham was PB 304's sister aircraft, PB 303, flown by Flight Lieutenant Parry who landed his aircraft at 1020, a little ahead of Flight Lieutenant Taylor and Wing Commander Piercy who both landed at 1035. There were large time differences in the arrival of the aircraft as for most of the morning the weather remained bleak and dominated by low cloud, so some pilots held off. By 1100 hours the conditions had slightly improved to record 9/10ths cloud at 1,000 ft and 10/10ths at 1,500 ft with a 15 knot wind. One by one the remaining Lancasters arrived overhead the airfield - Flying Officer Merideth's crew at 1125, Flying

Officer Fyson's P for Peter at 1150 and collectively nineteen crews returned a total of 334 x 500 lb general purpose bombs back to Metheringham.

A long silence now followed as the ground crew and operations staff waited for PB 304, the only outstanding aircraft. The intelligence officers only hung around for so long before they packed up and left. Listening to the crackle of static in the speakers of the control tower, the duty watch waited to hear the words, "Coffee Stall...Coffee Stall...this is Had None S for Sugar!" Every time the phone rang it might be expected that a person on the other end of the line, would confirm the bomber had landed at another station. The calls never came and in the operations room, the slot recording its landing time remained blank until at some point around half past twelve, someone would have written in the words "Missing".

Not all airmen on 106 Squadron heard about the loss of PB 304 straight away as the news was only slowly circulated around the crews and ground staff. Those who immediately became aware of the loss were its ground crew and the senior NCO in charge of "B" Flight, Sergeant Rasmussen. There were two empty dispersals and one aircraft from each flight missing, but by late Saturday afternoon Flying Officer Kitto's LM 215 had returned to base and only the one where PB 304 normally parked remained empty. This was an ominous indicator of the tragedy which had befallen Flight Lieutenant Lines' crew and if airmen from another crew had been sharing a room with those from PB 304, they could not have failed to notice that their possessions had been taken away and all signs of their presence almost clinically removed.

The job of clearing missing airmens' bedspaces and lockers fell to men from the Committee of Adjustment who were normally Royal Air Force Policemen and members of the Provost Branch. A note, that could only have been recovered from the flight clothing locker of Sergeant Raymond Barnes, records the crew's operational flights, including the last fatal one on 30 July. It is seemingly Raymond's own personal account of the operations he and his colleagues had completed and one can not help but feel he left it behind deliberately. The last entry is dated, "30.7.44. Troop concentrations Cahagnes Normandy (Daylight)". Only after he had attended the early morning flight briefing could Sergeant Barnes have possessed such information, although the note contains an obvious mistake that cannot easily be explained. At the top of the small piece of paper, Raymond had written, "Ops M ZU S for Sugar". The letter M clearly stands for Metheringham but the 106 squadron code letters were ZN. His crew were only allocated

"Sugar" on their second operation, so this suggests the flight engineer began his personal record on or after 18 July. We will never know why Raymond kept such a record and it is not beyond doubt that he had a bad feeling about the operation and wrote the notes in a hurry, as a testament to the operational record of his crew. With an eye for detail it was not like him to make mistakes unless he was being rushed and it remains a mystery.

When Flying Officer Vic Cuttle heard about the loss of PB 304 he remembered that the officer with whom he had chatted over breakfast on the morning of the operation, was the aircraft's pilot. Vic had recently returned from leave and while he was away several new crews had been posted in. Amongst them the officer who had sat opposite him in the mess admired his medal ribbon and said, "I see you've been on ops before?" Flying Officer Cuttle explained that it was the 1939-43 Medal Ribbon and he had flown Bostons in 1942. His colleague across the table smiled and remarked, "Well I hope I last that long!" Vic Cuttle thought no more about the conversation until he heard that Flight Lieutenant Lines and his crew had failed to return. Only a few weeks later the wireless operator, who flew in Squadron Leader A.L. Williams' crew, was himself shot down and, as one of the few survivors from his aircraft, spent the remainder of the war in a prisoner of war camp.

Those crews who were left behind had neither the time nor inclination to dwell on incidents where their comrades went missing, each dealing with the possibility of early demise in their own way. Some left spare cash behind with a member of their ground crew or in the mess, on the clear understanding that if they failed to return the money was to be used for a binge at a favoured pub at the earliest opportunity. Former Sergeant Rasmussen said he was regularly given wallets to look after and for a short while, sometimes, he was potentially the richest man on the station! The majority of aircrew only had a small number of colleagues with whom they closely associated which normally included room mates, who were often members of one's own crew, and those close friends from training days who had shared early experiences of service life. Everyone knew it did not do to mourn too seriously, because tomorrow it might be their names on top of a letter being written by the CO. These uncertainties they found bearable in the company of trusted friends; they had learned very quickly to live for the hour and took each day as it came.

OPERATION BLUECOAT

The fate of the 21 Lancasters from 106 Squadron

	Serial No	Fate
1.	ND 682	Lost 16 December, 1944.
2.	JB 663	S.O.C. 1946. *(after 111 Operations)*
3.	PB 298	Crash Landing Sept, 1944.
4.	PD 214	Lost 6 October, 1944.
5.	PB 248	S.O.C. 1947.
6.	LM 215	S.O.C. 1947.
7.	PB 191	S.O.C. 1947.
8.	PB 145	S.O.C. 1947.
9.	PB 281	Missing December, 1944.
10.	PB 203	Lost 12 Sept, 1944.
11.	JB 593	Lost 30 August, 1944.
12.	PB 303	Lost 17 November, 1944.
13.	PB 304	Crashed Salford July, 1944.
14.	PB 284	S.O.C. 1951.
15.	LL 948	Lost 15 March, 1945.
16.	LM 211	S.O.C. 1945.
17.	ND 868	Lost 24 Sept, 1944.
18.	PB 296	S.O.C. 1947.
19.	LM 641	Lost 8 August, 1944.
20.	PB 232	S.O.C. 1948.
21.	ND 331	Lost 30 August, 1944.

S.O.C. * Struck Off Charge

Chapter 6

A COMMUNITY IN CRISIS

In many of his paintings the famous Salford artist L.S. Lowry portrayed drab scenes of the city's mills and factories, often depicting its people as "match-stick" beings in an industrial colourless world. What his paintings fail to reveal however is the pride, courage, and determination of its citizens especially in times of crisis. From the day that the first German bomb dropped on Salford on 29 July, 1940, and during the blitz that followed, its people were resolved not to be beaten.

Salford like most cities in Britain raised money to build aircraft and during the week of 15 May-22 May, 1943, the City's Savings Committee set a target of £1,000,000 for 18 Lancasters and 35 Beaufighters. On Saturday, 15 May, the "Wings for Victory" Appeal was launched with a huge parade, involving the Central Band of the Royal Air Force, as well as units from local RAF stations and the Air Training Corps. At 3.00 pm no less a man than Major-General Ira C. Eaker, DFC, Commanding General of the United States Eighth Army Air Force, took the salute in Peel Park, accompanied by the Mayor of Salford, Councillor C.J. Townsend, JP.

Throughout the week events were held involving exhibitions and displays by RAF personnel and in Peel Park, the fuselage of a Lancaster was put on display, along with a Miles Master and a barrage balloon. On 20 May there was a parade and inspection of Women's Auxiliary Air Force units from Bowlee, Ringway and Wilmslow. On 22 May a Wings for Victory Dance was held at Broughton Senior School organized by 319 Squadron of the Air Training Corps, after a huge Youth Movement Parade involving the ATC, Sea Cadets, Home Guard and Army Cadets.

There is no way of knowing whether the Lancaster that arrived over the town a year later on a quiet Sunday morning was one of those sponsored by Salford's Savings Committee. Exactly how the ill fated bomber arrived over Salford will always remain a mystery, but from various reports and sightings, we can build up a picture of its last few minutes in the air. Approaching Manchester from the north-west at about 8,000 ft the Lancaster flew close to Oldham, Prestwich and Middleton and PB 304 was over these towns when the first signs of trouble appeared. With the aircraft losing height rapidly and its pilot no longer in full control, some attempt had to be made to salvage the situation, since Flight Lieutenant Lines knew ahead of him lay the Pennines, a long chain of hills with several peaks above 1,000 ft. On 7 August, 1942, an American B17 had crashed into Winter Hill near Bolton, while just over a year later, on 12 November, 1943, a Wellington bomber on a training flight crashed on Anglezarke Moor, to the north of Winter Hill, killing all six of its crew.

There were sightings of an aircraft which could have been PB 304 flying close to the Manchester Ship Canal near Irlam and, as the canal follows a straight line from the west coast near Liverpool to Manchester it would have made a good landmark to navigate by under difficult circumstances. Irlam is slightly further south of track than what might be expected if the aircraft was flying from Blackpool, but Flight Lieutenant Lines could easily have veered off course while attempting to keep his aircraft under control and he may also have been searching for a suitable landing site. If the Lancaster did in fact fly down the ship canal then it must have passed close to Barton Airport, the original Manchester Airport which opened in 1929. There is no suggestion that Peter Lines tried to land there because he may have judged the airfield to be much too small for an aircraft encumbered by a full bomb load to have a realistic chance of landing safely.

Barton Airport is built on Chat Moss over which runs the Manchester to Liverpool railway, built by George Stephenson in 1830 on ground which is known to be extremely soft and gave railway engineers many problems when they first laid the track. Hence it is possible that such limitations of terrain were in part responsible for Barton's modest development as an airport although only a short time before it had served its purpose admirably for a more fortunate crew when on 25 April, 1944, Lancaster PD 290 landed there by mistake. The captain, Flight Sergeant Crawford, shouted out of his window, "Is this Ringway?" and discovering his error shut down the engines whilst the crew took lunch. To take-off again they needed the help of a tractor, to hold the aircraft back until it developed full power. Then enterprise was rewarded as Barton's runways just proved sufficient to enable the aircraft to become airborne.

The problems the crew of PB 304 experienced developed suddenly and gave the pilot no opportunity to find a suitable airfield at which to land. The urgency of the situation can be seen from the fact that the crew could not fly their stricken aircraft as far as Ringway, nor did it have the power to fly to Woodford, where Avro Lancasters were assembled. This suggests the trouble struck suddenly and without any warning and there is evidence to indicate that an engine fire, or a fire in part of the fuselage was responsible. To fly to either Ringway or Woodford the bomber would have had to pass over the centre of Manchester and Flight Lieutenant Lines could not take that risk because of the potential threat to the heavily populated area.

At approximately five minutes past ten and whilst working in his garden, Mr Stanley Roberts of Kings Road, Prestwich, heard a loud "swishing" noise overhead. Looking up he could see nothing through the low cloud, but he was convinced it had been a large aircraft approaching from the direction of Heaton Park. The park was only a short distance away, and according to Mr Roberts the source of the sound moved in a westerly direction. At his place of work Mr Roberts had trained as a roof spotter and had knowledge of sound detection, speed assessment and elapsed time. When the aircraft flew over, he claimed the cloud base was no higher than 1,000 ft. From what he heard Mr Roberts got the distinct impression, that the source of the noise was trying to get beneath the cloud, but he could not hear the sound of its engines.

The silence of the four Merlin engines could have been due to the fact that the pilot and engineer were experiencing problems with the fuel cross-feed system, since with a wing on fire it would have been necessary to transfer fuel to the tanks in the other wing. Fuel management was largely the responsibility of the flight engineer and if there were problems with a booster pump or locating the cross-feed cock a temporary loss of power might have occurred. The cock was located in an awkward position on the floor behind the main spar and in an emergency it could be difficult to find and operate.

At the same time, a Mr Hunterman was attending a morning parade with his local unit of the Home Guard on Moor Lane. Just after the parade began he and his colleagues were rather surprised to hear the sound of an approaching aircraft and it slowly got nearer to their position before disappearing into the distance. Because of a high wall surrounding the grounds where they were parading, nobody saw the aircraft and most people thought it to be a German raider. However, very soon afterwards they heard a loud explosion. Just a short distance away Mr Ferguson lay in bed at his home in Oaklands Road, when he heard an aircraft go thundering overhead and thought it to be so low that it could easily have taken the roof off! This prompted him to jump out of bed and run to the window only to discover that the aircraft had already disappeared from view into the distance. Some minutes later, he heard a great explosion and returning to the window, Mr Ferguson saw a huge column of black smoke rising into the air from a site somewhere near the River Irwell.

Jack Howlett was only five years old in 1944 but what he saw that Sunday morning remained fixed forever in his memory. He was in the company of a young girl who lived near his home and they were walking to St Aidan's Church Sunday School together. They had got as far as the junction between Bradley Avenue and Cheadle Avenue when a large aircraft roared overhead flying very low - so low in fact, that the wash from its propellers blew the bonnet off the girl's head, compelling her to chase it down the road. The aircraft seemed to be heading for the playing fields on Littleton Road and although he did not know what type it was he clearly remembered that an engine or part of the wing seemed to be on fire.

It seems possible that Peter Lines might have considered an immediate landing on the playing fields. But a major problem for the pilot at this point concerned the angle of his approach which orientated towards one of the narrowest areas and would not have given enough space for a landing run, as it was very close to the river's edge. The fields were also covered with piles of stones, rubble and old vehicles, which had been put there in 1940 because of the then realistic threat of invasion from the air. Indeed two former Salford City Tramcars had been abandoned at the eastern end of the fields, which if not immediately in the Lancaster's path, certainly lay quite close to where it might have rolled.

Flight Lieutenant Lines could not have been fully committed to making a landing and in the event the Lancaster made an extremely low overshoot. It could have been a baulked landing but it gave the pilot a final opportunity to survey the ground, to which he had been guided by his engineer, Sergeant Barnes, who lived locally. The Lancaster climbed away from Littleton Road Playing Fields to cross the River Irwell in the vicinity of the weir, narrowly avoiding a collision with the steeple of St.George's Church on Whit Lane. Gladys Keever who lived in Cook Street, witnessed the scene from her own doorstep, as the aircraft struggled to gain height across Charlestown as it flew towards the rising ground of Pendleton. Near Halton Bank the bomber turned steeply to starboard through approximately 140 degrees and PB 304 was then heading back towards the Irwell to approach the playing fields for a second time, but now on a more suitable bearing which would maximize the available space.

There are reports that as the Lancaster flew over Halton bank, three men were seen sitting huddled inside the rear door, as if ready to jump, and seven year old William Mackin who was playing in Charles Street when the aircraft passed overhead claimed it was engulfed in flames. While in the company of two friends, eleven year old Christopher Rose heard the loud roar of aircraft engines, as they walked near Summerville Road on their way to St.Luke's Church in Swinton Park Road. His friends Dave and Vinny Green walked on but Christopher stopped to look for the source of the noise, straining his senses as he scanned the overcast sky but failed to immediately catch sight of the aircraft as the sound disappeared into the distance.

He ran down Charles Street watching the blazing aircraft as it descended into the valley and saw it go down towards a position he described as a few hundred yards upstream of Jubilee Bridge. In Whit Lane, Hugh Yates, who had observed the aircraft flying around earlier on, was amazed to see it return: this time passing very low above his home in Dumville Street. It skimmed the roof-tops of houses in Wellington Street, Armitage Street and Indigo Street, narrowly avoiding another collision with the 200 ft chimney of the Whit Lane Soap Works, known locally as "Soapy Toms" to continue its flight path over Pendleton Colliery on a course roughly parallel with Langley Road.

Mary Hassall was at the kitchen sink of her home in Dixon Street, scraping some carrots for the family's Sunday lunch when she heard a loud noise and looking up saw a large aircraft, which appeared to be heading directly for her - an experience shared by fourteen year old Joyce Bowles on the steps of her home at 16 Langley Road who stared in disbelief at what she saw. A large aircraft was "lit up" as though on fire, heading straight towards the row of houses where she stood, coming from the direction of the railway line and across the Manchester to Bury canal. Though she knew the dangers, Mary Hassall continued to watch the aircraft as it passed above the roof-tops from right to left, totally fascinated by the unnerving sight. Chris Rose only spotted the aircraft during its final moments in the air, recalling that as it hit the ground the Lancaster appeared to bounce and sit on its nose for a few moments before exploding. William Mackin witnessed the explosion from Charles Street and Hugh Yates, who had run up Langley Road trying to follow the aircraft, heard a terrific bang just as he neared Regatta Street. From the moment the aircraft hit the ground the seven crew were almost certainly doomed.

It was not unknown for aircraft carrying bombs to make successful crash landings without them exploding, but few ever survived the type of violent impact that befell PB 304. The Lancaster's airframe was built to withstand an impact equivalent to its sudden arrest from approximately 12 ft per second or about three times its own weight, before breaking up. As its impact with the ground would have almost certainly exceeded these limits it is likely that the bombs were thrown from their racks and exploded because of the inertia forces to which they were subjected. Chris Rose suggested the bomber might have hit the ground first with wheels down before being flung onto its nose and in this event some of the impact would have been absorbed, but hardly materially increased the odds in favour of the crew's survival. Mary Hassall who had one of the best views of the bomber's final moments claimed she saw the port wing dip into the roof of a house in the next street and that must have badly damaged the aircraft. It is a tribute to the skill of Flight Lieutenant Lines, that he maintained control for another 70 yards as his crippled Lancaster flew towards the river-bank.

It is difficult to put a precise time to events concerning the incident: Stanley Roberts is certain that the noise that he heard and presumed to be the stricken aircraft, passed over his house at precisely 1005 hours; whereas the call from the air raid warden informing the authorities of the disaster was recorded at Swinton Incident Centre at 1010 hours. Taking it into account that it would have taken anyone at least two minutes to compose themselves after such an event, reach a phone and make the call, we can time the crash at approximately 1008.

The houses on Langley Road, immediately behind the scene of the crash, took the full force of the blast and suffered varying degrees of damage. All the houses lost windows and slates were thrown from roofs. Inside many homes, ceilings collapsed and doors were blown off their hinges in a turmoil of utter devastation. Regatta Street suffered more than most and one house was reduced to rubble, as a result of the collapse of its gable end wall. The roof and upstairs floor also fell in but amazingly 61 year old Mrs Harriet Chase and her daughter Florence, managed to avoid serious injury, being later dug out of the wreckage that had been their home and taken to hospital where Mrs Chase was detained for observation. The house next door to the Chases was also badly damaged; with the occupants, John and Annie Reeves being treated for cuts and shock resulting in 65 year old Mr Reeves being kept in Hope Hospital.

Technically the incident happened within the boundary of Swinton and Pendlebury, though the border with Salford was less than fifty yards away. This part of town has always had closer associations with Salford and since 1974 the area has been part of that city but the Incident Control Centre for the Borough of Swinton was then based at Swinton Town Hall and had responsibility for organizing and liaising with the emergency services in this district. National Fire Service

Headquarters in Salford received notification of the crash at 1014 and within four minutes two appliances from "D" Division were on their way supported by two ambulances and a car dispatched from Victoria House in Swinton at 1020.

Hugh Yates claimed to be among the first to arrive on the crash site and was amazed at how little of the aircraft remained in recognizable form. On the river-bank a large impact crater had formed surrounded by pieces of twisted metal which lay scattered over a wide area. Pockets of smoke could be seen rising from the ground accompanied by the sound of small detonations which Hugh later learned were caused by exploding ammunition from the bomber's .303 calibre machine-guns.

Mr Hunterman and the two dozen or so members of the Home Guard from Moor Lane received notification of the disaster very quickly and were ordered to get across to Langley Road as soon as possible. He confirmed that nothing remained of the bomber but small pieces of wreckage and the odd bit of burning material though they dutifully guarded the crash site against unauthorized intrusion until police from Swinton and Salford forces arrived to set up a cordon preventing public access. Throughout the boroughs of Swinton and Salford vibrations from the explosion shattered windows and shook buildings.

Ten year old Jack Garry who lived in Littleton Road ran across the playing fields towards the river where he and several other boys searched the debris for a souvenir. Amongst the remains he was stunned to see a black and white cow, lying dead. He realized that the animal probably came from Austin's Farm at the northern end of the playing fields which used the fields for grazing. It did not take Jack long to discover a small panel with some instruments on it which he thought looked like part of the aircraft's main panel in the cockpit. Picking up the object Jack was about to walk off with his prize when he heard someone shouting at him. Unfortunately he had been spotted by an alert policeman who demanded that he put his find back again where he found it!

One of the first serious casualties of the accident was Mr George Morris, who had been working on his allotment with his wife, Caroline, on the other side of Langley Road at a considerable distance from the where the aircraft had crashed. George nevertheless received injuries caused by shrapnel or wreckage which had been hurled several hundred yards by the blast. Caroline was not hurt and after obeying her first instincts in support of her husband, despatched her son George to inform her brother-in-law what had happened. Meanwhile

Mr Morris was made as comfortable as possible by family and neighbours until an ambulance arrived to take him to Salford Royal Hospital, accompanied by his sister Elsie and Mary Wardle, who herself had been badly cut by flying glass. At the hospital doctors discovered that Mr Morris' injuries included a fractured femur with other serious wounds to his leg and stomach.

Joseph Bamford, my father, was in bed when the Lancaster crashed and the first thing he knew of it came when the back bedroom windows blew in. Splintered glass showered the room and though he tried to save himself, diving under the blankets did not prevent him being badly cut. Still suffering from shock he staggered downstairs only to find his 72 year old mother badly injured. My grandmother had been standing in front of a window and taken the full force of the blast, getting peppered with broken glass. Lucy already had a heart condition and the shock alone could have been fatal. She was taken to Salford Royal Hospital and detained for treatment and observation.

Most of the ambulances travelled to Langley Road from Victoria House in Victoria Park Swinton a little over two miles away, but delays were caused because of the number of people who needed treatment. At first none but the most urgent cases were treated or taken by ambulance and many had to find alternative transport including Joyce Bowles, who remembered how she and a few others had to travel in an old open cattle truck which belonged to a Mr Rowe. She said it smelt terrible but with so many injured people there was no other way to get to hospital and even Albert Phillips of Regatta Street, who had serious injuries to his eyes, was obliged to commit himself to this unsavoury mode of transport.

Most residents who had been indoors when the crash happened suffered some degree of cuts or bruising, from being flung against walls or doors forced open by the blast. Mr Walter Pike and his wife Nora, were about to sit down to breakfast in their home on Langley Road when suddenly windows were smashed and doors disappeared, as everything flew across the room in a blast of hot air. The breakfast which had so recently been placed on the table, vanished in the debris and together with Mr James Partington, his father-in-law, Mr Pike was fortunate to require treatment for only cuts and shock.

People living on the other side of the River Irwell along Littleton Road escaped the worst effects of the blast, although most families had relatives or friends living on Langley Road and many of their number flocked over Jubilee Bridge to offer assistance or find out about those they knew. Leslie Green lived near The Racecourse Hotel at the town end of Littleton Road and his family was convinced that the explosion had been caused by a flying-bomb. His friend James Bold lived on Langley Road and the blast threw his mother from the kitchen at the back of the house, through to the front door where she broke her arm. Like many others that Sunday morning Mr Bold, was enjoying a lie-in and he fortunately escaped injury.

Some of the houses were so badly damaged that the properties had to be classed as uninhabitable by the Borough Surveyor who was one of the first officials on the scene. Rapidly he made an assessment of the extent of the damage so that immediate plans could be put into action for temporary repairs to some twenty houses, which were said to be no longer fit for habitation. The stunned occupants began quietly to move their furniture out. In disbelief they piled up treasured possessions on the pavement or on the opposite side of the road. Within a short time all the frontages were full of wardrobes, tables, chairs and carpets - the belongings that had, only moments before, characterized their private and seemingly unassailable home-life.

Ken McNee who worked at the local Universal Metal Products factory, witnessed the devastation just a few minutes after the crash happened and recalled that all the windows were smashed and some people were staggering about covered in blood looking dazed. Residents tried to help each other and the women in particular rallied round, giving what assistance they could and making pots of tea, while others comforted the injured.

There is a gap in the Swinton Incident Room Control Log between 1030 and 1145 which suggests that after the immediate flurry of activity, even the authorities arrived at a point where they did not know what to do next. The Salford Incident Centre did not receive formal notification of the crash until 1148, although it is hard to believe its personnel had not already been informed. At 1145 Councillor Townsend received permission to use the Whit Lane Rest-Centre so that over the next twenty-four hours this was to become the focal point for social contact, providing hot meals and pots of tea for residents and rescue workers. Mrs Chase was taken there after being dug out of the remains of her home in Regatta Street and somewhat revived by a hot mug of tea spoke to reporters about her ordeal: "I was in bed at the time", she told them, "I heard a plane and shouted to Florence, 'Here comes a flying bomb!' Suddenly there was a terrific crash, the bed began to tilt towards the window. Then glass tore the bedclothes as the windows came in. I saw the roof sagging and screamed. I don't remember much more until I found some men helping me into the street".

88

6. Sgt Mohand Singh (Rear Gunner).

7. Sgt Arthur Young (Wireless Operator).

8. Sergeant Robert Saul wounded five days earlier he missed the last flight of PB 304.

9. A crew picture taken at 1661 Heavy Conversion Unit May 1944, shortly before their move to 106 Squadron.

SALVAGE SCENE

INSTEAD of spending a quiet Sunday morning yesterday, a number of residents of Pendlebury had to salvage their furniture and effects from houses damaged by the bomber crash, as these "Daily Mail" pictures show.

MISSED THE CHOIR OUTING

To Repair London

By Daily Mail Reporter

TOMMY BENNET, 25, a bricklayer from Wigan, leant against the stone entrance pillars of one of the large houses in a London square, titled over his eyes his new blue felt hat with a red feather, and said: "It's grand to do a bit of lounging—this is the first day off I've had in a month."

Tommy Bennet is one of hundreds of workmen who have come to London from all over the provinces to repair flying-bomb damage.

They have been working a 12-hours day, from 7 a.m. to 7 p.m., seven days a week to repair tiles and windows of bomb-blasted homes.

The square where they live resounds now only to men's voices in a dozen different dialects.

They are all here, the dreamy-eyed Irish, the gay lads from Lancashire, the big, quiet Scotsmen, and some ruddy-faced, soft-voiced men from Somerset.

They sit on the steps of the houses eating bread and cheese, lettuce, and meat pies done up in a cardboard box for fivepence until the great kitchen in the square is finished.

'Bolton is Cleaner'

Thomas Morris, 53, a carpenter from Bolton, says: "London's a dirtier place than Bolton." For the first time in 43 years he missed the choir outing at the parish church.

"I wrote to vicar," he told me, "and said I couldn't get, but that I hoped my wife would go in my place, because I'm wanted here."

"So vicar wrote back and sent me the parish magazine. I'm going to read it now with my bit of dinner."

Unloading new bricks from a lorry on the green-overgrown gravel paths was Frederick Sharp, a labourer from Manchester. He used to live with his mother.

"I suppose we're here for the duration," he remarked. "But the W.V.S. are looking after us fine."

A concert was given last night to the repair squads by grateful Londoners. It took place in the square.

Flew With Enemy, Shot One Down

A Mustang pilot joined a squadron of Focke-Wulf 190's thinking they were Mustangs after a sweep in the Carteret-Le Mans area. Two minutes later he realised the plane nearest him was a German—so he turned into it and shot it down.

Note.—The main differences between Mustang and F-W are in wing shape and engine appearance. The Mustang has a pointed nose, the F-W 190 is radial.

Jive Experts Wear Out U.S. Pianos

From Daily Mail Correspondent
NEW YORK, Sunday.

THE "jazz and jive" fever now sweeping the United States is wearing out so many pianos that a major crisis has arisen in the piano-making industry.

Manufacturers cannot cope with the rush of orders they are receiving from "Jazz and Jive" clubs which have spread all over the country.

One company recently received on one day enough orders for remodelled pianos to fill 11 freight cars.

Young members of these clubs glory in the name of "Hep Cats," "Rug Cutters," and "Boys and Girls of the Bobbysock Brigade."

The piano-makers complain that they hit the keys so hard during their "jam sessions" that they need specially strengthened models.

The War Production Board has given its blessing to the output of pianos so long as it does not interfere with war production. But the fever is rising so high that with reduced staffs manufacturers cannot make pianos fast enough.

R.A.F. Help Out Vicar

R.A.F. officers preached the sermon and conducted services from Langham Parish Church, Norfolk, yesterday so that the vicar, the Rev. H. Jackson, could take charge of the reception of evacuees from London

A HEAVILY damaged house and (inset) a welcome break for sandwiches. Below: The shopkeeper tidies up.

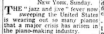

The Village of Champion

10. Page from the Daily Mail which reported on the damage caused when PB 304's bomb load exploded on impact, killing two people and injuring over 100.

Harriet Chase and her daughter Florence were two very lucky women.

As members of the community waited for news of the injured and contemplated the arrangements expected of the authorities, they stood around chatting nervously, smoking, telling jokes, and trying to make light of the morning's events. At 1205 Swinton Council's Town Clerk gave instructions to the Town Yard about the removal and storage of furniture although there seems to have been some delay in carrying out this work, probably caused by residents who were hesitant about allowing their property to fall into the council's charge. It was later agreed where their possessions were to be stored however and the bulk of property was finally sent to Buile Park for safe-keeping in the building which now houses the Mining Museum. Being a Bank Holiday weekend, many people had gone away to Blackpool and North Wales: record queues blocking the entrances to Manchester's railway stations and at Victoria thousands seeking a brief respite from the constraints of wartime jostled to get on the trains.

The Womens' Voluntary Service (later to become the WRVS) arrived to help out and quickly organized facilities to prepare hot food and drinks, since with a large number of Civil Defence and rescue workers being drafted in there was a demand for a constant supply of hot food. The two National Fire Service vehicles remained on the scene until just after mid-day and although they had arrived within four minutes of receiving the call-out at 1018, this immediate response could never have saved the aircraft's crew. The size of the fire was recorded as being small thereby confirming that after the initial explosion little remained except small amounts of burning debris.

Peter Evans played rugby league for Swinton and was part of a team that contained some of the greatest players the game has ever seen - men like Bryn Evans, Harold Evans and Martin Hodson, the latter made famous by his 75 yard record goal kick. On the morning of the crash however Peter was in Salford Royal Hospital, having undergone an operation on his knee. He worked for Gerrards, a large joinery construction company based in Swinton, as did quite a number of Swinton players in those days because the firm offered a convenient arrangement which allowed time off for training. Raymond Barnes had worked at Gerrards prior to joining the RAF, so he and Peter had been good friends, meeting up each morning at the top of New Street to walk to work together but as a result of Raymond's service career Peter had not seen his old friend since 1937.

Salford Royal Hospital is about two miles from where the Lancaster crashed but its buildings were still shaken violently by the explosion from its bombs and Peter Evans along with other patients wondered what had happened, especially as soon afterwards doctors and nurses visited the wards to make arrangements for extra beds. All non-serious cases were quickly moved and other patients shuffled around to other wards but because he was a private patient paid for by Swinton RLFC, Mr Evans did not get moved and ended up in a ward on his own.

When the newcomers arrived, Peter saw that they were in an awful state with most of them being covered in dust and dirt from head to toe and the nurses found it difficult to cope with such a large intake and so asked the patients to help perform some of the more routine tasks. In response, Peter along with other patients provided the new arrivals with drinks whilst generally looking after them as they waited for treatment, and from talking to people he learned something of what had happened. At that stage however he had no idea that his former workmate was involved and it was not until a considerable time later that he discovered Raymond had been on board the aircraft.

By 1305 fifty-three casualties had been reported, fourteen of whom were admitted to hospital and amongst the people detained in Salford Royal were Robert Dutton; Jane Atkinson; Harriet Chase; Ellen Hotchkinson; George Morris and my grandmother Lucy Bamford. A further six were taken to The Royal Manchester Eye Hospital, including Albert Phillips and John Barnes.

John Barnes was a very good friend of my father and they played football and cricket together for Langley Road, which had its own teams competing in local leagues. For John Barnes, the day the aircraft crashed brought misery, darkness, and an abrupt end to his sporting days or to any chance of living a normal independent life in the future. John with his wife Eva, lived at 36 Langley Road and he had just started two weeks' holiday, from John Shaws, an engineering company in Broughton and like many other families they had been sitting down to enjoy Sunday breakfast when a truly appalling noise shook their home. Eva having their second child on her knee immediately put her head down to protect the two of them, while the windows shattered and glass flew into the piano behind her. John unfortunately looked up and splinters of glass blew into both his eyes so that when Eva next looked at her husband, she saw his eyes only as (in her words) "pools of blood". Eva who was six months pregnant started screaming, as the house was in ruins, her badly injured husband only a few feet away from her and she was approaching total shock. Thankfully her mother-in-law was upstairs with the eldest child and between them they managed to get John outside where the policeman on the spot turned out to be Eva's brother, who lost no time in arranging for an ambulance to take them to Salford Royal Hospital.

At the hospital they were preceded by a long line of people who all had injuries of various degrees, waiting to be attended to and Eva could not face it any more, so she retired to the visitors' waiting room where after a while she saw her policeman brother again, who confirmed that John would have to go to the Royal Manchester Eye Hospital for specialist treatment. There being nothing more she could do, Eva returned home on a tram and was surprised to find Whit Lane cordoned off at the bottom. Her mother-in-law had disappeared but a policeman suggested she look in the rest-centre which proved good advice and after they had become reunited the police helped out again by taking them to Eva's oldest brother in Partington Lane Swinton. While they were there they received news that surgeons had operated on both of John's eyes, indeed on one of them twice and although the bandages could not be removed for at least three weeks, the prospects of John seeing again out of either eye were thought to be minimal.

At some point during the day representatives from the Royal Air Force arrived and two commissioned officers requested they be taken to the crash site. Hugh Yates who had earlier witnessed the final moments of the aircraft in flight, was an ARP messenger based at Wellington Street School and being in the building when the officers turned up, was instructed to take them up to Regatta Street and show them around. It is most likely that the airmen were from the Aircrew Dispatch Centre at Heaton Park, which was less than three miles away and their job was to supervise the examination of the wreckage to identify the aircraft from what little remained. They would also have made arrangements for guarding the site and removing the debris. By checking serial numbers on large components like engines, a positive identification could be made and since four other Lancasters were missing the process of notifying next of kin could not begin until this vital task had been completed.

Later on in the day when they had started to recover, residents talked about their experiences and began to speculate as to what had caused the tragedy. Some spoke to reporters about what they had seen, as in the case of Home Guard Company Sergeant-Major Harry Tiddeswell, who said he was one of the first to arrive on the crash site, having seen the aircraft during its final moments in the air. He reported he had seen the plane straggling behind a formation flying in an easterly direction when "Suddenly", he claimed, "the engines began to splutter. Then flames and thick black smoke poured out of it, as it dived down on us with pieces dropping from the fuselage. I shouted 'Duck!' We flung ourselves down as it loomed over us and it gained enough height to skim the house tops then banked steeply as if trying to land on Salford Playing Fields".

Mr Samuel Foy of Langley Road said he was standing on the tip further down by the river bank when he noticed an aeroplane flying towards him from the direction of Manchester, heading towards Swinton. He estimated that it was only about 100 ft high when it banked to the right, as if trying to land on Littleton Road Playing Fields, but as he watched it the aircraft suddenly dived straight into the bank of the tip, at which point Mr Foy said the crash caused the earth to quake violently and the ensuing explosion blew him through the opening of Dixon Street into Langley Road.

A lot of people said they thought the sound of the explosion was made by a V1 flying-bomb which is hardly surprising as during the previous six weeks London and the south-east of England had come under constant attack. Though news of the terror weapon had reached the north, the press did not report where they landed, in order not to aid German intelligence but by the end of July most people were aware of flying-bombs and became convinced that Manchester would be the next target. Like London, it had received a terrible pounding during the blitz years and the people of Salford had not yet put the particularly devastating Christmas of 1940 out of their minds. It was far easier for many people to accept that a flying-bomb had landed than believe what had actually happened.

Some witnesses told *The Salford City Reporter* that they had seen the aircraft flying around, but it had only come to their attention after passing very low above Pendleton, heading towards Littleton Road. They claimed it was obviously in some kind of trouble but it looked as though the pilot was doing everything he could to avoid hitting houses in his path and according to the newspaper reports some pieces of the aircraft were found over half a mile away from the crash site.

One man who witnessed the effects of the explosion and subsequent blast was walking past the newly opened offices of the NSPCC, on the corner of Dumbell Street and Station Road in Swinton which is approximately two miles away from where the bomber crashed. Mr Blower, on his way to Christ Church on Bolton Road for the morning service had heard aircraft flying over all morning, but it was rather misty and he had failed to see them through the cloud. Mr Blower claimed that the large plate glass window in the NSPCC building vibrated and bulged out of its frame but just when he thought the glass was going to shatter, it shrank back into its frame, to return to its normal shape. At the time of writing the NSPCC offices are still there and one of the few buildings in Swinton which remain in use for their original purpose.

The Mayor of Salford, Alderman Leonard Webb, lived only a short distance away from Langley Road in Orchard Street off Whit Lane and his own home was damaged in the same way as many others in the surrounding area. He quickly paid a visit to the crash scene in an attempt to organize aid and was impressed by the way that the police, Civil Defence and rescue workers got on with things. In a statement to the press he also praised the pilot and crew, "On behalf of the citizens", he expressed appreciation, "for the devotion and skill of the pilot and crew of the plane. We deeply mourn them and recognize but for their action in guiding the plane away from the centre, many lives might have been lost". There is little doubt about Alderman Webb's sincerity as he saw the incident as both a personal tragedy and one which concerned the City of Salford and its people. Within a short space of time he had set up a fund on behalf of The Royal Air Force Benevolent Organisation, raising money by selling copies of a specially commissioned poem which describes how the crew struggled to make a safe landing. The poem was written by J. Belshaw of Pendleton.

He circled here, he circled there,
This pilot high up in the air,
Looking for somewhere, but in vain,
To land his almost done for plane.

His thoughts were for his gallant men,
Who had been on "Ops" and back again,
With a fully laden bomber craft;
T'was enough to send this pilot "daft",

When he thought of the houses down below,
He was doing his best to miss them though,
He tried to reach a playing field,
With nothing to help him or act as shield.

So praying to God, he made a bold bid,
No hero's done better than this man did,
But something appeared to hit a wing,
And sent him reeling with a swing,

93

Into the side of a darned old tip,
Which he might have cleared with an extra flip.

But it wasn't to be and this man died,
Along with his gallant crew beside,
So let us remember as long as we live,
These men for us, their lives did give,
There was only two died among us all,
God needed them both and gave them a call,
So they could give thanks to the pilot and crew,
From the people below, over whom they flew.

During the afternoon at 1445, Mr Hartley Shawcross the Regional Commissioner, visited the crash site. He had been the Commissioner for the north-west area since the beginning of the war and in certain situations he had the powers to take full control. The Commissioner also co-ordinated between local authorities and government departments. After speaking to members of the rescue squads he inspected damaged properties and chatted with residents in an attempt to reassure them about some of their concerns. Escorting him during his visit the Mayor of Swinton, Councillor J.H. Jones, praised Civil Defence workers for their hard work and particularly acknowledged the part played by Senior Warden Farmer, whom he claimed had been a "Tower of Strength". By the time the commissioner left in the late afternoon the number of casualties stood at 66 injured.

By 1515 hours the aircraft had been positively identified as an Avro Lancaster and the fact that it had crashed with a full bomb load was entered into the log of the incident centre. In the community all sorts of rumours had begun to circulate about the type of aircraft involved in the crash and the purpose of its mission. One story claimed that the aircraft had taken-off from Woodford on a test flight and it had got lost before crashing, after having run out of fuel. To some extent this was a prophetic guess since a short while later a Lancaster did crash on a test flight, though nowhere near Salford.

Exactly how PB 304 S for Sugar was identified is not known, but once this confirmation had been received by The Air Ministry, a process began which would lead up to the families of the crew being notified of the bad news. When the Air Ministry received news that a "Missing" aircraft had crashed at a known location, 43 Maintenance Group were informed about it and details were relayed to salvage teams working in that particular area. In places like Linconshire where

94

crashes occurred as part of daily life there were many teams working all over the county, but in those regions with fewer airfields where crashes were less frequent, personnel had to be drafted in from the nearest maintenance unit.

The nearest one to Salford was 35 Maintenance Unit based at Heywood near Middleton which received and dispatched engines as well as other major aircraft components, so it should have had the necessary equipment and manpower needed to perform such a salvage operation. There were others in the area at Wilmslow and Handforth but they were many miles away. PB 304 was listed as Category E which meant that the engines and airframe were a total write-off and no parts from them could be used again.

A procedure for the disposal of Category E wreckage was laid down in memo 43G/1592/E dated 20 June, 1940, which required that a team of fitters and armourers examined the wreckage and removed any sensitive equipment the aircraft may have been carrying. Armourers searched the wreckage for any bombs or bullets and large items like engines were recovered with a Coles Crane, if the crash site was accessible - whereas the engines of aircraft which crashed on the moors miles from anywhere were often buried on site, or if in mountainous terrain were left to rust, thus affording a grim reminder of the past. According to some witnesses at least two of the engines from PB 304 were found in the River Irwell and they had to be recovered, along with the other fragmented pieces to leave the crash site clear and safe. In cases such as the crash at Salford other work had to be done and this included the search for unexploded bombs and the bodies of the seven members of the Lancaster's crew.

By 1630 hours Swinton Council had sent round 20 men and two vans to carry out first-hand repairs, under the supervision of the Borough Surveyor. In most cases repairs were only superficial to protect the houses from bad weather. Windows were covered with felt and roofs had tarpaulin sheeting thrown over them, to cover holes where slates had been blown off. Although only twenty houses were declared uninhabitable, many people chose not to return to their homes and 150 camp-beds were made available at the rest-centre. However most of these remained empty because the majority of people preferred to stay with family or friends who lived nearby.

Towards the evening a Civil Defence reserve column arrived on the scene with fully equipped vehicles and extra manpower. Parts of the Lancaster had penetrated deep into soft ground around the river-bank and a considerable amount of excavation was necessary to recover certain pieces of wreckage. The land had originally been used as a tip but in more recent times men played pitch-and-toss on the croft and boys were given a sixpence to look-out for the local bobby. Now the shape of the ground was changing as rescue workers dug deep in a desperate final bid to recover the remains of the cockpit and fuselage.

At just after 2000 hours something happened that caused a bit of a panic and at 2010 the rescue squad received an urgent message, for all available personnel to attend the crash site as soon as possible. This message was passed through Swinton Incident Centre but the exact nature of the emergency is not clear, though entries in the log book give a clue. At 2300 hours the all clear was given by the bomb disposal squad and it seems possible that at least one bomb may have failed to explode. If an unexploded bomb was found, that in itself still does not explain the need for additional manpower, since in such a situation it would have made more sense to have less people around and all none essential personnel evacuated. The other possibility is that a vital part of the aircraft containing the remains of the crew became unearthed and extra help was required.

This seems to have been the beginning of a flurry of activity on the crash site since at 2100 hours the mobile canteen returned to the incident centre, but at 2255 hours Senior Warden Farmer, under instructions from the Town Clerk, requested that it should be made available again and it returned to Langley Road. At one point it seems possible that a decision to stop work for the night had been made but in the light of some new circumstances, the authorities decided to continue with work all night.

During the evening the fire-brigade had been in the locality again dealing with a chimney fire at 3 Regatta Street which was the home of the Phillips family who like many others had moved out of their house earlier on in the day. Albert Phillips said it probably started because his father had a habit of building huge fires, even in the summer so that soot and dirt loosened by the explosion probably fell down the chimney breast causing it to ignite. The same thing had also happened at 22 Whit Lane and in fact for the previous two weeks "D" Divsion had dealt almost solely with domestic fires caused by such things as faulty wiring and cigarette ends. A serious fire at Magnesium Electron in Clifton on 25 July proved an exception, when 9 tons of magnesium drums started to burn after being ignited by sparks from a welding torch.

The subject of what was discovered of the airmens' remains is a sensitive one, but is hard to avoid in view of overall events. A signal sent from 106 Squadron to the Headquarters of The Royal Canadian Air Force gives the clearest account: "Bodies of Flying Officer Reid, Sergeant Davenport and Sergeant Singh recovered. In view of circumstances of crash and that it is not possible to recover any more bodies, the deaths are being registered in accordance with A.P. 1922, paragraph 185, of the remaining members of the crew." On RAF Form 39 it states that Flying Officer Reid's body was not recovered until Saturday 5 August and his death noted as being caused by "Multiple Injuries".

For purposes of identification airmen wore discs around their necks containing only name rank and number: a similar disc was also worn on the left breast of the battle jacket. Between the flying brevet and the pocket was sown a strip of leather with the airman's name on it but sometimes a more personal object was used to identify an airman, as in the case of Sergeant John Davenport, who was recognized by a watch, that had been bought as a present by his wife Irene. That three bodies were found supports the claimed sighting of three men sitting in the rear door of the Lancaster as it flew above Halton Bank just a minute or so before it crashed. We can only presume that they were waiting to parachute to safety but the Lancaster was below 900 ft and too low for them to jump.

During the early hours of Monday morning The Air Ministry began its task of notifying the airmens' next of kin. A telegram sent to the parents of Sergeant Raymond Barnes was timed at 0355 and its contents are very brief but to the point.

"Deeply regret to inform you that your son R. Barnes missing from operation 30th July. Letter follows."

When Raymond's mother heard the explosion from her home in West Drive, she thought there had been an accident at the Wheatsheaf Colliery where her husband Harold worked, but later in the day she heard about the air crash and that evening Raymond's younger sister Irene, was taken down to Langley Road by some neighbours. They had a car and offered to take her for an evening drive, but first went to see what was going on at the crash site. At that point neither Irene nor her parents had any idea that Raymond was involved in the incident and one may imagine their disbelief and profound shock as they connected the telegram's message with what she had seen the evening before. Raymond's parents later received a letter from 106 Squadron's Commanding Officer, Wing Commander Piercy which he wrote on 2 August, giving further details of the loss of the crew. Over the next few weeks the Barnes family received several messages containing expressions of condolence including letters and cards from The Air Ministry,

Swinton Council and King George VI from Buckingham Palace. The latter was a simple but sincere message:

> "The Queen and I offer you our heartfelt
> sympathy in your great sorrow.
> We pray that your country's gratitude for
> a life so nobly given in its service may
> bring you a measure of consolation."

On Monday the search for bodies and wreckage continued but switched to the water when police frogmen dragged the River Irwell which is not particularly deep but in some places flows quite fast and any debris or remains may have been swept downstream towards Manchester. During the previous weeks a lot of rain had fallen and the winding course of the river together with nature's ability to create strong currents, was enough to swallow up forever, most objects in its path.

In the early hours of Tuesday morning the first civilian death occurred as a direct result of the Lancaster crashing, when George Morris passed away in Salford Royal Hospital at 3.45 am. A preliminary Inquest was held at Pendleton Town Hall on 2 August and the circumstances of his death were confirmed by the Deputy Coroner, Mr H.S. Holmes. Forty-five year old Mr Morris was said to have been in good health prior to being injured by the aircraft crashing and having attended Wellington Street School, was later employed by Salford Cleansing Department where he had worked for a number of years. The Deputy Coroner adjourned the first hearing and a full Inquest held on 16 August when the cause of death was given as "Pulmonary Embolus, following a fracture of the left femur, as a result of a Royal Air Force aeroplane crashing into the ground". The verdict was recorded as Accidental Death.

At lunch-time on Tuesday The Mayor of Swinton met The Mayor of Salford at the Whit Lane Rest-Centre, just before it finally closed down at mid-day. Mutual thanks were exchanged for the co-operation between the departments of the two authorities and both men expressed gratitude towards the rescue workers, many of whom were still on the crash site. But behind the public image, there were certain differences of opinion between the two civic leaders about the actions of the pilot and whether it had been really necessary for him to try to land in such a built-up area. It is claimed that Alderman Webb suggested the pilot be recommended for a gallantry award but Councillor

Jones had other views.

The Mayor of Salford suggested that the pilot be awarded The Victoria Cross for his part in preventing a greater loss of life, similar suggestions having been made in the past, when doomed aircraft narrowly avoided crashing into a residential area. In August 1940 a Blenheim of 600 Squadron flying from Manston in Kent suddenly appeared out of the clouds, then narrowly skimmed the roof-tops before diving into the sea just outside the harbour. The people of Ramsgate believed that the pilot had done exceptionally well to avoid a terrible tragedy and a campaign began for Flying Officer Grice to be awarded a decoration for gallantry.

Alderman Webb's proposal may have originated with something that had recently been highlighted on a radio programme and in many national newspapers. In "The Radio Padre's Programme" broadcast on 11 July, the Reverend R.Selby had talked about the life of Pilot Officer Cyril Barton, a young pilot recently awarded The Victoria Cross and who had flown Halifaxes with 578 Squadron at Burn. On the night of 30/31 March, 1944, he went on operations to Nuremberg and his aircraft was attacked several times by fighters, but despite terrible damage to his aircraft and the fact that some of his crew baled out because of a communications problem, he carried on to bomb the target. On the return flight Barton had to force-land his Halifax at Ryhope, just south of Sunderland in circumstances similiar to those encountered by Flight Lieutenant Lines at Salford. It is possible that Alderman Webb heard the programme and became influenced by its emotional content since there were a number of factors against any award for gallantry being made to Flight Lieutenant Lines, not least that there were no witnesses to tell what really happened on board PB 304. The drafting of the citation would therefore have presented something of a problem.

On Tuesday afternoon the incident was raised in The House of Commons by Mr Robert Cary, Member of Parliament for the Eccles Ward when by a written notice he asked The Secretary of State for Air if he had any special statement to make about the British aircraft which had crashed at Langley Road Pendleton. Giving his reply, Captain Harold Balfour, Joint Under-Secretary of State for Air, said the aircraft in question crashed while returning from operations and the cause of the accident was being investigated. "I am sure", said Captain Balfour, "that the House will wish to join me in expressing sympathy with the relatives of the crew and with those who were injured, to whom we wish a speedy recovery".

While thanking his Right Honourable and gallant friend for his answer, Mr Cary continued to press Captain Balfour on the issue of compensation and asked, "Will the War Damage Commission admit full liability, as if the incident had occurred as a result of direct enemy action? Secondly, out of a total number of casualties 14 persons are detained in hospital seriously injured. If any person suffers total or partial incapacity or is injured in any way and deserves compensation, will the Ministry of Pensions deal with the case as though the injury had been sustained as the result of direct enemy action?" Captain Balfour said he could not answer the questions because they were matters concerning the Chancellor of the Exchequer and the Ministry of Pensions respectively.

This did not satisfy Mr Cary and he then asked who the individual could appeal to if any dispute arose over decisions about financial problems arising from the incident since as he pointed out, working people could suffer great hardship if there was any delay. Various MPs got involved in the debate and a Mr Pethrick asked that the Chancellor of the Exchequer approach the War Damage Commission to, "Point out that this aeroplane was struggling home as a result of direct enemy action!" Damage he said was caused by enemy action if only indirectly. Mr Pethrick's positive statement saying that the aircraft was struggling home as a result of enemy action is interesting and one must wonder what the source of this information could have been. Presumably he would not have said such a thing without some form of evidence to support it and regardless of the substance of his claim, within a few days the Minister of Pensions, Sir Walter Womersley, agreed to Mr Cary's demands.

My grandmother Lucy Bamford died on 14 August at my Aunt Alice's home in Tennyson Street Salford, after being discharged from Salford Royal Hospital on 3 August. Lucy was unhappy in hospital but was only allowed to leave after there had been a slight improvement in her condition. At her daughter's home, Lucy spent the last few days of her life surrounded by family and two grandchildren, Eric and Doreen. An Inquest held on 16 August declared the cause of death to be heart failure due to Myocarditis, accelerated by injuries and shock received as a result of a Royal Air Force aeroplane crashing near her home. This resulted in a verdict of "Accidental Death". She was buried in Agecroft Cemetery on 19 August.

At a meeting of Swinton Town Council on 18 August, it had resolved that the Town Clerk should forward a letter of condolence to the relatives of those who had died as a result of the air crash. Regardless of this letter and many other expressions of sympathy, sincere as they were, my father still felt bitter that the family received only five shillings compensation for his mother's life. She was old and had been ill for some time but even under those circumstances the miserly sum was an insult. No amount would have made up for her loss but the amount that now equals 25 pence was hardly one day's pay for a labourer even in 1944. Overall the appeal system allowing the injured to complain about the amounts of money they were awarded failed to work.

The amounts awarded to others were generally small though they did vary widely: Joyce Bowles for instance received only twelve shillings and sixpence whereas Elsie Atherton was given £24. Fifty years after the crash Joyce's scars remain visible but the mental suffering is not so obvious and she has never flown because of a fear of aircraft, rather than just a fear of flying. Even modern jets which pass close to her home on the flight path into Manchester Airport make her nervous, all because of something which happened on a cloudy Sunday morning in 1944. The widow of George Morris, Caroline, was given a small pension, as were certain other people who were injured like Albert Phillips and payments were calculated in proportion to the nature of the disability and in lieu of the loss of earnings.

Below is the list of casualties given by The Ministry of Defence which contains several known errors. It was composed and categorized by the MOD and I understand it may not be complete. Wherever possible I have corrected those listed wrongly and apologize for any mistakes.

KILLED
Lucy Bamford, George Morris

SERIOUS CUTS & SHOCK
Harriet A. Chase, Robert Button, Jane Atkinson, John Hughes, Joyce Bowles, Eric Bowles, Audrey Bowles, Freda Brown, John Reeves, Lillian Tomlinson, John Barnes, Albert Phillips, Irwin Stancliffe, Ellen Hodgkinson

SERIOUS CUTS
Agnes Hughes, Eric Atkinson, Joseph Gorton, Annie Bowles, Joseph Bamford, Walter Rushton, Elizabeth Rushton, Edna Rushton, Elsie Atherton, Barbara Jones, Mary A. Healy, Jessie Richardson, Phoebe Lomas, William Aitken, Edna Farmer, Joseph Dudley, Edna Wilmot, Fred Thomas, Walter Pike, James Partington, Eva Barnes, Tom Birchall, John White, Elizabeth Birchall, Albert Hodgkinson, Annie Hodgkinson, Nellie Lang, Maud Bold, Eliza Atherton, Catherine E. Ashcroft, Mary Wardle, Sarah Ellis, Sydney Phillips, Edna Phillips, Dorothy Phillips, Annie Reeves, W. Edge, Eliza Edge, Martha Hassall,

Robert Hassall, Raymond Williams, Ethel Wallwork, James Wallwork, Florence Evans, Kenneth Kenyon, Tessie Cuttings, Violet Cuttings, Derek Cuttings, William Hodgkinson, Alice McBain, Elsie Christian, Shirley Christian, Bertha Moores, Henry Birchall,

It can be readily observed how many families had more than one member injured but the full extent of this is partly hidden by the obvious fact that married women carry their husband's surname. Through marriage the Chase, Lomas and Morris families were all related and the Bowles, Phillips, Hodgkinson and Birchall families were particularly hard hit. Elsie Christian the sister of George Morris, had a six week old daughter, Shirley, and she was the youngest amongst the injured. The oldest was 90 year Mrs Mary Healey.

Most injuries were caused by flying glass but several people had limbs broken after being thrown through the air by the blast, whilst others were badly bruised and most residents suffered varying degrees of shock. 17 year old Air Training Corps Cadet, Kenneth Kenyon, received his injuries when the shock-wave blew him off his bicycle as he peddled down Littleton Road on his way to morning parade although at the time he must have been at least half a mile away from where the Lancaster crashed. Property in the area of Littleton Road was damaged though not extensively and only a few residents were injured on the other side of the River Irwell.

The Ministry of Defence list contains the names of 70 casualties but newspapers such as the *Daily Telegraph* claimed that over 100 people had been injured and this is probably nearer the true figure. It is not known exactly how the figures were calculated, but it is quite likely that they included only those who attended hospital and received treatment and, quite a number of residents did not seek medical attention, except that given by family or friends for a variety of reasons. Before the National Health Service was set up in 1948 people feared that if they went to hospital or consulted a doctor they would inevitably get a bill and have to pay.

General reporting of the incident by the media was good, considering wartime restrictions and censorship of the press but none of the newpapers reported the widely held view, and as claimed by Mary Hassall, that the bomber probably struck the roof-tops prior to crashing. The suggestion was rather that the damage to Mrs Chase's house occurred as a result of the blast from the explosion and it is understandable that immediately after the disaster few people were concerned about the details of what had happened, when most were just happy to be alive.

The press played down the extent of the damage caused to properties in the community and also the length of time that most of them would remain uninhabitable. According to a report in one newspaper, repair work was well under way by the Sunday evening and it was considered that residents would be able to return to their damaged homes almost immediately. The reality of the situation turned out very differently however and most did not go back to live there for many months. Mary Wardle and her husband for instance went to live in Stretford and their home was not made available to them until 17 March, 1945; nine months after the Lancaster had crashed. Even then Mary and her husband found themselves in an impossible situation over their belongings which the council would not release until they moved back into the house! Mary wanted them handed over prior to them returning to their old home but it seems that the entanglements of bureaucracy prevailed and the fears of some residents about letting the council get hold of their things appear to have been realized.

The majority of houses on the Langley Road rows were privately rented but some belonged to Andrew Knowles & Sons, who owned Pendleton Colliery and the amount of time taken to repair inevitably causes one to wonder what kind of haggling took place between the council, landlords and government, as to responsibility for compensation and payment for repairs. It would conceivably have been an ideal opportunity for the landlords to re-negotiate their tenancies and get the properties refurbished at government expense.

The events of a single day in July 1944 influenced the futures of many people and left physical and mental scars that remained with a number of former residents for the rest of their lives. Albert Phillips was just 17 years old when he not only lost the sight of one eye but any prospects of pursuing his ambitions to become a professional driver. He already had a job driving waggons for a local company and on the Friday before the incident picked up his first load, leaving the lorry parked nearby, in readiness for delivery after the Bank Holiday weekend. On the Sunday morning Albert awoke early to take his dogs for a walk but the weather was so miserable that he decided to go back to bed. He lived in the same row of houses as Mrs Chase on Regatta Street, and when the bomber flew above his home, like John Barnes he instinctively looked up and caught some slivers of glass in his face which cost him the sight of one eye.

On several of its previous operations, PB 304 had lifted a 13,000 lbs bomb load and had it carried that weight of explosives on 30 July more lives might have been lost and the area totally devastated. There were those who argued that regardless of the skill of the pilot or the bravery of the aircraft's crew, they should never have attempted to land in a built up area. The critics who perpetuated such debate had almost certainly never struggled with the controls of a damaged aircraft, or had to make split-second judgements concerning their own lives or those of six others. The decision to take the action that he did, was probably the most difficult that Flight Lieutenant Peter Lines ever made.

Chapter 7

THE MYSTERY REMAINS

The six targets for Operation BLUECOAT were chosen by Air Chief Marshal Leigh-Mallory, who was the Commander-in-Chief of the Allied Expeditionary Air Force. Orders were transmitted by teleprinter from Bomber Command Headquarters High Wycombe to group head-quarters on the Saturday night at 2125 hours. There the staff deter-mined the strength of each squadron under its command and how many serviceable bombers they might have available and orders also included the amount of fuel to be uplifted, times over targets, details of aiming points and bomb loads.

106 Squadron had recently lost two aircraft: Flying Officer Pemberton's crew in ME 778 O for Orange had failed to return from Stuttgart and LL 953 C for Charlie, was so badly shot up when it land-ed, it had to be taken off the line for major repairs. Even so 106 man-aged to get 21 Lancasters serviceable to add to the total of 184 aircraft dispatched from 5 Group and this figure includes a single Mosquito from 627 Squadron based at Woodhall Spa.

Originally 5 Group had assigned 207 aircraft but 21 were cancelled and a single Lancaster returned early with engine trouble; 1 Group allocated 155 aircraft but in the end dispatched only 104. Both 3 and 6 Groups sent 99 aircraft, 4 Group managed to put up 101 and the Pathfinders from 8 Group raised 30 Mosquitos and 75 Lancasters. This was despite a signal from Bomber Command HQ, sent during the early hours of the morning, requesting squadrons to send as many aircraft as possible, because the army were committed to attack.

Detailed orders contained on operation Form "B" Number N0335, did not mention anything specific about the crews having to return their bomb loads should they fail to see their aiming points, but they did strongly emphasize the need for accurate bombing. In the case of markers being obscured crews were instructed to aim at the upward edge of the main smoke concentrations. Where the order to return the bomb loads originated is not known, but it was impressed upon the crews at briefing, despite the fact that some airmen ignored it later in the day and the most likely sources are the squadron commanders or the Air Officer Commanding 5 Group, Air Vice-Marshal Cochrane. If Flight Lieutenant Lines had jettisoned the bombs from PB 304, then he would have increased his crew's chance of surviving a forced landing and the 18 x 500 lb bombs were a critical factor causing their deaths.

Pilots who found themselves in difficulties near built-up areas had to make instant decisions and quickly weigh up the risks to their crew as well as those on the ground. Air Chief Marshal Harris the Commander-in-Chief of Bomber Command, had very strong views on how pilots should respond in such situations and the kind of action they should take. In 1940 Harris wrote to Cochrane, who at that time was Air Officer Commanding 7 (OTU) Group, stating that it should be made clear to pilots that as trained airmen - they were more valuable to the community than either the cost of their aircraft, or civilians who might be killed if they crashed.

According to Harris pilots should not attempt to land unless they had a 75% chance of getting down safely and they had no right to keep members of their crew aboard unless they had a 99% chance. The cost of a Lancaster in 1944 was approximately £40,000; to train an airman £10,000, so to lose a Lancaster with seven trained men on board cost in excess of £100,000. Despite the huge amounts of money involved this was almost certainly not an exercise in economics but Harris trying to preserve the numbers of aircraft and lives of his crews. It does seem rather arrogant though for him to have suggested that an airman's life was any more valuable than that of a civilian, who just happened to be unfortunate enough to be under his flight path. For a pilot to abandon his aircraft in a situation where it would fall on those beneath him, would have been considered by most airmen as a callous and grossly unprofessional act. No officer would ever hope to enforce such a regulation.

To give him due credit, "Bomber" Harris was genuinely concerned about his crews and he played a leading role in ensuring that they received the best training before being sent on operations. The operational training units and heavy conversion units were started as a result of Harris' repeated campaigning for better trained airmen but he also fought hard to ensure the new types of aircraft had the best in modern navigational and bombing aids, to guide them with greater accuracy, to and from the target. Arthur Harris had been amongst the first airmen to realize the potentially destructive power of aircraft in the bombing role, believing firmly that given the right equipment, excellent results could be achieved. Harris however did not have a lot of faith in the ability of his crews or equipment to carry out "Precision" bombing and this partially restricted the role of Bomber Command until it came under the control of SHAEF in April 1944.

It was somewhere in the north-west where Flight Lieutenant Lines first got into difficulties and although he was not immediately prepared to abandon his aircraft he needed to land, regardless of the odds. There might have been a time when at least some of the crew could have baled out but for whatever reasons, none of them did. Unfortunately in the area where he found himself when the emergency arose there were fewer airfields available than in many other parts of the country. The three main emergency diversion airfields at Manston, Carnaby and Woodbridge, with their long runways and crash facilities were all on the south-east and east coast. Woodbridge in Suffolk was heavily used by aircraft returning to bases in Cambridgeshire and East Anglia and a lot of aircraft from 3 Group landed there after the BLUECOAT Operation.

He had already left the security of Blackpool's Squires Gate airport behind and it seems that his Lancaster did not have the power or capability to return to it. It is reasonable to assume that his aircraft was unable to fly the relatively short distance to an airfield at Woodvale and we have already established that the Lancaster was not airworthy enough to reach Ringway or Woodford, with the result that during the vital moments when he urgently needed to land, there was nowhere to go and Flight Lieutenant Lines had to improvise.

It was rare for aircraft flying on operations to pass over Manchester but the region was on a training route used by 106 Squadron and its crews regularly flew in the vicinity of the city. Warrant Officer Jim Cunningham had flown over the region on 8 April, 1944, as part of a Birmingham - Bristol - Manchester - Goole cross-country exercise and a few days later he did the same again. Some former 106 Squadron airmen have suggested that as they were in the vicinity, Flight Lieutenant Lines was about to perform a "beat up" of his flight engineer's home in West Drive Swinton and that accounts for their crashing so close to where he lived. After all several pilots had been guilty of performing similar stunts including Flying Officer Kitto and Flying Officer Merideth, who had both recently "buzzed" the homes of airmen in their crews.

Whilst there is no denying that during their last meeting in June, Raymond Barnes had told his younger sister, Irene, that if his plane should ever pass overhead, he would wave a white handkerchief out of the window, it is highly unlikely that this was anyone's intention on the day and the truth is that it was pure coincidence that the bomber ended up so close to Sergeant Barnes' home. In the event it would seem logical that the best person to have directed Flight Lieutenant Lines was the flight engineer, who seems to have used his local knowledge in the hope of saving himself and his colleagues. If we take into account the fact that several witnesses claim the bomber was on fire, the decision to take such drastic action appears to have been a last resort. The Lancaster, as suggested by statements made in Parliament, might have been damaged by enemy action, or its performance affected by a simple mechanical failure. Theories as to the cause of the tragedy are endless, but the probabilities can be narrowed down to a small number of explanations. However as we know Peter Lines was not the kind of officer to take such risks and simply following the recommended routing as advised by 5 Group, that theory does not seem feasible.

PB 304 was built at Avro's Chadderton Factory in the spring of 1944, as part of a batch of 800 Lancasters, under contract number A/C 1807. There are many stories relating to the workforce at Chadderton but none so often told as the one about the young man who frequently complained of low pay and long hours. When he went to see the General Manager, Roy Dobson, he was shown an adjacent room with a bed in it and told, "I'm here twenty-four hours a day!" The man left the office somewhat embarrassed and he never did get his pay rise. Workers put in a hard day's labour, as they did throughout the rest of British Industry, and the average pay at Chadderton was only £2 10 shillings a week. 3,050 Lancasters were manufactured at Chadderton in Bay 3 and during the war the workforce peaked at over 11,000. As the fuselage of each Lancaster neared completion it was broken down into four main sections and transported by road to Woodford nearly twenty miles away. The pieces were reassembled, the wings and engines fitted, and the aircraft test flown before being delivered to RAF squadrons by pilots of number 14 Ferry Pool of the Air Transport Auxiliary.

The final assembly of PB 304 took place in early July and its engines were installed on 5 July. The date of its first flight is not known, but details of its sister aircraft PB 303 which also went to 106 Squadron are available and confirm that PB 303 was test flown on 8 July. This information is recorded in the log book of former Avro flight engineer Eric Allan and it is logical to assume that PB 304 went through at about the same time.

Test pilots like Jimmy Orrell and Syd Gleave took the Lancasters up for two flights of approximately twenty minutes duration when the performance of each aircraft was assessed so that any change of trim or balance could be carried out prior to its delivery to the RAF. Every tenth Lancaster off the production line was subjected to a terminal velocity dive, to test the airframe at speeds of up to 375 mph. It was during such a flight that something went terribly wrong and on 11 September, 1944, PB 579 dived vertically into the ground a few miles south of Woodford. Syd Gleaves was flying the aircraft and by coincidence the flight engineer was again named Barnes: Harry Barnes. It is thought that a fuel jettison pipe worked loose from the wing, stripped the elevators and deprived of all means of corrective control - the Lancaster buried itself into the ground.

From Woodford, Lancasters destined for 106 Squadron flew to 54 Base at Coningsby, where over one hundred modifications were carried out to the electrical, bombing and navigation circuits. Eventually many of the modifications were picked up by Avro and carried out during initial production but 54 Base continued to take aircraft on charge for the four units under its control - 83, 97 106 and 617 Squadrons. The latter had been based at Woodhall Spa since January 1944, while 83 and 97 Squadrons flew from Coningsby. When Lancasters arrived they were assigned to a particular squadron before the riggers painted the unit codes and individual aircraft markings, in large white letters on the fuselage. PB 304 was taken on charge by 106 Squadron on 11 July and became "ZN - S".

Lancasters PB 303 and PB 304 were delivered on the same day and replacements in lieu of the five aircraft lost on the operation at St Leu d'Esserant on the night of 7/8 July. For some reason there had not been a "Sugar" on the squadron since May and the serial number of the previous Lancaster to bear this letter was LL 891 which had been delivered to Metheringham on 26 March, 1944. On 7 May it took-off at 2210 hours to bomb an ammunition dump at Salbris and was one of seven aircraft lost out of the force of 58 which attacked the target. It went down with eight men on board but its skipper, Flying Officer Penman, had a second pilot that night, Flying Officer Steylaerts who was undertaking his first and last operation.

Throughout the war several different versions of the Lancaster were produced including the Mark IIs with Bristol Hercules air-cooled engines and Mark Xs, made in Canada by a subsidiary company of Avros, Victory Aviation. PB 304 was a mark BIII and had Rolls-Royce type 38 engines, produced by the American motor manufacturer, Packard. The company had been pursuaded to build aero engines by Lord Beaverbrook early in the war after Ford had refused to co-operate. A Packard Merlin was equivalent to the Rolls-Royce 22 engine and the main differences were that they had American screw threads and Bendix carburettors. To begin with, Packard engines were very popular with engine fitters because they were delivered with special tool kits, which became status symbols and as a result frequently went missing! This soon created problems because it was difficult to work on Packard engines with standard Imperial tools. Without the American kits, fitters were forced to work on engines with normal spanners, which had a tendency to round-off corners on nuts and resulted in grazed knuckles, so generating a lot of bad language. The only other option was to borrow someone else's tools and so the cycle continued. Some pliots and engineers claimed that Packard Merlins were inferior to Rolls-Royce built engines but there is no evidence to support this bias and their performance level should have been equal.

Servicing standards on all squadrons were generally high and ground crews worked hard in all conditions to ensure that the maximum number of aircraft could be dispatched. One of the line chiefs on 106 Squadron's "B" Flight, Sergeant Rasmussen, said that because they were young nothing was beyond their capabilities and the ground crews coined the expression: "The difficult we do immediately....the totally impossible takes a few minutes longer....have a smoke while you wait!" The average working week was about 90 hours and they had to eat whenever the opportunity arose, regardless of where they were. On one occasion he caught some of his airmen boiling up a stolen chicken, in a drum above a sand and petrol fire. The bird had been "won" from the local farmer and as the price for his silence he demanded a leg from their prize!

Despite being damaged by flak on 25 July while returning from St Cyr, PB 304 did fly on the night of 26/27 July but was then grounded for the Suttgart operation on 28 July. Minor repairs were frequently carried out on the line so PB 304 could not have been too badly damaged and only anything more serious than Category "C" went back to 54 Base at Coningsby, or in cases of extreme damage, the Avro Repair Depot at Bracebridge Heath near Waddington. On the operation to Givors on the night of the 26/27, PB 304 bombed from a lower altitude than many other aircraft and it is possible that Flight Lieutenant Lines may not have been satisfied with the performance of his aircraft's engines. After that trip the aircraft remained on the ground for three days before it flew on another operation, although it was test flown prior to departing on 30 July. A lot of work was carried out on PB 304 in that time and, its pilot Flight Lieutenant Lines was ultimately responsible for it being airworthy before taking it on operations. Before taking-off on 30 July the last thing he did was to sign the standard RAF Form 700 to accept the aircraft and acknowledge any work done on it, or fly with minor snags that he considered acceptable.

Sergeant Laurie Rasmussen, knew the men and machines better than most having worked on 106 Squadron for most of the war and having gained experience of several different types of aircraft, including the Handley Page Hampden. After fifty years he had only vague memories of the incident involving PB 304 but recollected the fact that R for Robert and S for Sugar arrived on the same day. Mr Rasmussen was puzzled about the the incident at the time because most accidents happened during the phases of landing or take-off and rarely occurred in flight. After the war he got in touch again with many former crews from 106 Squadron, including some taken as prisoners of war and to his credit, and that of his groundcrews, nobody reported losing their aircraft through mechanical failure, other than those failures caused by enemy action.

If we disregard for now the possibility that straightforward mechanical failure caused PB304 to crash, the only other logical conclusion is that the aircraft was damaged by some form of enemy action. The chances of the Lancaster having encountered a fighter are slim, though they cannot totally be ruled out. Bombers on the BLUECOAT Operation were supported by 216 Spitfires of the Allied Expeditionary Force from 11 and 83 Groups and Christopher Buckley reported that the fighter escorts could be seen quite clearly through broken cloud, merrily milling around far above the bombers. Other similar types adding weight to Allied numbers were PR Spitfires from 542 Squadron and Flying Officer Ibbotsen in MD 213 performed sweeps taking photographs between Caumont and Le Havre from 0845 to 1100 hours.

Of the two air gunners aboard PB 304, Sergeant Singh was by far the more experienced having seen service in both turrets - a man whose presence might well have added to the crew's confidence and for him a daylight trip to France should have held no terrors. He had seen action on more than one occasion and flown above Berlin in the midst of the battle for that city. On the night of 22/23 April during an operation on Brunswick his aircraft was attacked by a fighter and Flight Lieutenant Holden put ND 331 G for George into a corkscrew to port, while Sergeant Hulme the mid-upper gunner, tried to get his guns to bear on the fighter. Sergeant Singh in the rear turret struggled to get a shot in because it attacked from the port beam and fired from a range of 250 yards. In the subsequent combat report Sergeant Hulme claimed to have hit the fighter with a sustained burst.

On 30 July German fighter pilots would have found it difficult to stay hidden in broad daylight long enough to make an attack. Only the pres-

111

ence of two German fighters was observed in the target area and they were an Me 109 and a Ju 88 (Air 14/3744). There was plenty of cloud below 3,000 ft, but up above the clear sky was dominated by Allied fighters, flown by enthusiastic young men who wanted a crack at the enemy before the war ended. The activities of the Luftwaffe though were not just confined to the coast of France and it is not beyond belief that a sharp eyed German pilot, on the lookout for a lone aircraft spotted PB 304 and made an attack somewhere over the Channel before being driven off by the gunners. What makes this theory less likely is that if his aircraft had been attacked and damaged, Flight Lieutenant Lines would have landed at the earliest opportunity at an airfield in the south of England.

The fact that many eye-witnesses claimed that the Lancaster was on fire does give a clue as to the possible causes of its demise. Fire was an element hated by all airmen so fear, panic and confusion were normal reactions. On board each Lancaster, stowed at strategic points were five fire extinguishers, but down each side of the fuselage ran ammunition trays for the guns in the rear turret and other inflammable materials. The very nature of bombers and their deadly cargos made them vulnerable to fire and many airmen had already learned this the hard way. On the night of 26/27 April, 1944, Sergeant Norman Jackson a flight engineer on 106 Squadron, climbed out on the wing of his Lancaster, in a desperate bid to put out a fire. Other crewmen hung onto the harness of his parachute but when it caught fire they were forced to let go and Sergeant Jackson fell to earth but survived despite suffering terrible injuries. Jackson was captured, hospitalized and then became a prisoner of war whereas ME 669 O for Orange crashed soon afterwards and several members of the crew were killed, including its pilot, Flying Officer Fred Mifflin. When his actions came to the attention of the authorities Sergeant Jackson was awarded The Victoria Cross.

If an engine caught fire and could not be put out with its internally fitted extinguisher, then normal practice demanded that a pilot should put his aircraft into a steep dive, so that the airflow could blow it out. If Flight Lieutenant Lines took this action it would go some way to explaining why the Lancaster was flying so silently and so low above Stanley Roberts' home in Prestwich and why it entered the Irwell Valley. If the fire broke out as the aircraft passed to the north of Prestwich, then the flight-deck crew might just have been trying to recover from such a steep descent in a bid to extinguish an external blaze.

The loss of an engine did not mean just the loss of propulsion but also essential services, upon which the crew relied for navigation and communication. For instance off the port inner ran a generator and main services hydraulic pump for the rear turret; off the port outer engine ran another hydraulic pump for the rear turret. Everything seems to point to the fact that the pilot was experiencing difficulties with the port (left) engines and the actions of Flight Lieutenant Lines support this view.

The Rolls-Royce Merlin engine is liquid cooled, unlike the air cooled Bristol Hercules, which powered some bombers. The system was designed to allow the engine to develop greater power and run for long periods but its weakness was the engine's dependency on the liquid coolant and the radiator through which it ran. Any leak or slight puncture could be enough to run the engine dry and within five minutes it might seize up altogether, so increasing the probability of fire. Generally speaking liquid cooled engines were more expensive to produce because their manufacture involved the use of more components and the position of the tank containing the coolant fluid (30% Glycol 70% Distilled Water) was in a particularly vulnerable place. Shaped like a horseshoe the header tank sat at the front of the engine air-intake, on top of the reduction gear and was easily damaged by flak, bullets or shrapnel fired from beneath it.

Another feature of the Rolls-Royce Merlin is its characteristic shape which compared with other engines is flat, with a surrounding stream-lined cowling to reduce airstream drag. The Merlin is commonly known as an "In-Line" engine because its cylinders are lined up behind one another in a "V" shape and coolant fluid comes into direct contact with the 12 cylinderbore liners whilst circulating through the engine block. On the two inboard engines air was diverted to a heater radiator in the wing and flowed close to a vent near the wireless operator's position. He normally complained it was too warm, while the rest of the crew shivered and froze. While a Lancaster sat on the ground the Glycol radiators often leaked and to the dismay of the electricians, coolant sometimes dripped onto the starter motors. In the air with the engines running they should have been sealed and coolant normally leaked only when an aircraft received some form of battle damage.

One of the most likely explanations of events on the morning of 30 July involving PB 304 could be that its coolant tanks were hit as it circled the Normandy Battlefield by splinters of flak shells, or damaged by machine-gun bullets. The initial damage might not have attracted the crew's attention at the time, until at some point during the flight, dials on the flight engineer's panel would show the coolant temperature moving dangerously towards the 140 degrees centigrade level. A gradual loss of coolant was often difficult to detect and I have heard stories from flight engineers who claim that sometimes the dials gave hardly any warning until it was too late. Failure to recognize early warning signs, if there were any, could result in an engine fire if it was kept running. A sudden loss of power on an aircraft loaded with bombs is exactly what might cause a pilot to look for somewhere to land.

The flight engineer's notes regarding damage by enemy action, instructed him to check all fuel gauges for abnormal consumption and if a tank indicated loss of fuel, or if the overall consumption seemed abnormal, all engines were to be run off the damaged tank until it was nearly empty. The booster pump in that tank was then turned on and the selector switches for those on the other side turned off. When the contents fell to 20 gallons the engineer was to change tanks again but if the pilot and engineer had other things to cope with, they could easily have been overloaded with more urgent tasks.

Damage that caused a fuel crisis is less likely because Lancasters were fitted with self-sealing tanks which gave limited protection from shrapnel. Each wing had three separate tanks, numbered 1, 2, and 3. Number 1 was situated nearest the fuselage, with number 2 between the fuselage and inboard engine and, number 3 outboard of the outer engine. A problem with the fuel system might have aggravated other defects and if the coolant system was damaged, it is likely the underneath of the wing was damaged as well. A fire in an engine or wing would also have necessitated switching tanks and juggling with switches and fuel cocks.

For the Bluecoat Operation the Lancasters of 5 Group had been uplifted with 1,500 gallons of fuel. The maximum amount carried without extra tanks was 2,154 gallons, so the Lancasters were filled to just over half their capacity and this would have been enough to keep the aircraft airborne for approximately six hours, depending on what boost and rpm the pilot used. Consumption of each aircraft varied slightly, but at 1000 hours PB 304 should have had at least 400 gallons of fuel on board, which added to the bomb-load and, not counting other military equipment, would give an all-up weight of approximately 12,000 lbs (5 Tons).

There is something unusual about the figures recording the number of hours each of PB 304's engines was supposed to have run. According to the Accident Report, filed on RAF Form 765 (C), three of them had run for five hours longer than the other remaining Merlin.

Listed below are the numbers of the engines fitted to PB 304 and the hours that are recorded. The first part of the engine serial number was allocated by The Air Ministry and the second part by the engine manufacturer.

PB 304 ENGINE NUMBERS & HOURS LOGGED

Engine	Engine No	Hours logged
Port Outer	A.17065/AF 42/A252061	56hrs 30mins
Port Inner	A.15578/AF 42/A250574	56hrs 20mins
Starboard Outer	A.16319/AF 42/A251315	56hrs 20mins
Starboard Inner	A.17405/AF 423/AF252401	51hrs 10mins

The difference could be explained by the fact that the starboard inner had been shut down in flight, but the airframe had only 51 hours and 10 minutes on it. The engines should have experienced more operating hours than the airframe because of running time spent warming up, ground taxi-ing and being tested by the engineers. Despite normal variations, five hours does seem a large discrepancy and the obvious explanation would be that the engine had been changed at some point.

According to RAF Form 465, all four engines were installed on 5 July and no changes took place after that date. The number of the starboard engine is slightly different from that of the other three engines but that in itself does not prove an engine change took place. There has to be some sort of explanation for the difference and a simple clerical error can not be ruled out. RAF clerks worked under pressure like everyone else and they were not particularly noted for their accuracy. The starboard inner had still done over 51 hours so that means if any change did occur, it happened quite early on in the aircraft's history.

An alternative theory, suggested by Dick Breedijk who has worked with the Dutch Air Force recovery team and has experience of engine numbers, is that PB 304 may have been originally built with a reconditioned engine. Because of engine shortages it was not unusual to fit those taken from Lancasters that had been involved in minor incidents. They were overhauled and returned to the assembly sheds and fitted to new aircraft.

Flight Lieutenant Lines was an experienced pilot and according to at least two of his instructors, an airman with exceptional ability. He did not have a great amount of time on Lancasters, but his overall total probably exceeded 1,500 hours and had the situation in the air been one that he could have salvaged, his aircraft would have flown to the nearest airfield. To get some idea of the Lancaster's performance on three and two engines the Pilot's Notes (A.P. 2062), provide a guide.

On three engines and with a bomb load, the Lancaster was expected to maintain height, at a speed of 145 mph; with two engines out it should have been possible to maintain height at 10,000 ft but only after the bombs had been jettisoned. There are stories of Lancasters flying the last leg to base on one engine, in a down-hill glide onto the runway but the crew of an aircraft with bombs aboard could never hope to do that and by the time the danger had been fully realized, any chance of getting rid of them had been missed. Regardless of what is written in instruction manuals, it seems logical to assume that Flight Lieutenant Lines was struggling to control the bomber on only two engines and if those engines were on the same wing, the automatic pilot would have ceased to function, making the aircraft very hard to control.

Having abandoned his south-easterly track, Flight Lieutenant Lines turned PB 304 onto a westerly heading somewhere near Manchester and the change of course was brought about by immediate emergency action. The aircraft passed close to Heaton Park, which is sited on high ground of between 350 and 400 ft above sea level and even if they could see the park it offered the crew no comfort despite its 600 acres of grass covered land since many Nissen huts were also strewn around the land. The undulating ground also featured a large boating lake and other obstructions, which would have prevented a Tiger Moth from landing let alone a four-engined bomber. From this or other familiar landmarks like the River Irwell, Sergeant Barnes recognized where he was and guided his skipper towards the only piece of ground available to them which was to become the crew's last hope.

Littleton Road Playing Fields cover approximately 29 acres of grassland being bounded by the River Irwell to the southwest and Littleton Road to the north-east. A Lancaster bomber needed something in the region of 1,400 to 1,600 yards for a normal landing run and the most Flight Lieutenant Lines could expect from the playing fields would be 800 yards, if he approached very carefully. After the first overshoot the bomber climbed out above the high ground of Pendleton and peformed a sharp banking turn to starboard.

The action taken by Peter Lines and the direction he turned the Lancaster possibly tells us what side of the aircraft the failing engines were on. During training on multi-engined aircraft pilots were taught to handle engine failures in a certain way. They were taught to fly with the good engines on the inside of a turn, so that during a banking turn using ailerons and rudder, the extra power would not force the aircraft out of control. If a pilot failed to observe this principle then the chances of his aircraft spinning into the ground dramatically increased and this may account for the reason that Flight Lieutenant Lines flew in the direction he did. With the exception of a few jinking turns towards the end of its flight, the only major manouevres performed by the aircraft seem to have been to starboard, suggesting that any problem lay on the port side. The fact that the port wing was said to have dipped just as the aircraft approached the houses on Langley Road also indicates a loss of power on the port side, which allowed the wing to enter a stall.

The official documents and reports on the loss of PB 304 contain a certain number of contradictions but do not really explain what happened. To some extent this is to be expected because of the large number of aircraft lost during the war. No government department was going to go out of its way to solve, what was to it, just another incident. When asked to do so, the MOD have replied to requests for information. In December 1991 I wrote to The Ministry of Defence and received a very brief summary of events.

"At approximately 1015 hours PB 304 was seen
to enter cloud, which was very low, and appeared
to be making for some open parkland. The port wing
tip fouled the river-bank, causing the aircraft to
crash into the river-bank and explode on impact.
Sadly all the crew were killed together with one
civilian on the ground. 69 other civilians were
injured. 70 houses and 3 work buildings were also
damaged".

Several eye-witnesses reported that the aircraft crashed after entering a near vertical dive, although not everyone agreed this was the case. One such claim was made by a Mr Lawrence Hamill, who watched the bomber during its final moments in the air from a position on Littleton Road and told reporters that he thought the aircraft had no chance of recovery. If Flight Lieutenant Lines did experience the loss of power on the port side, then a steep approach was made to maintain airspeed and prevent his aircraft from stalling. An acute angle of descent could easily be mistaken for the aircraft crashing in an uncontrollable dive. In the final moments Flight Lieutenant Lines would have had to have levelled out as he neared the ground and if he was aiming to make the playing field, the lower bank of the river on that side gave him an extra twenty feet. It is unfortunate that the speed fell off and his Lancaster approached a stall.

The Archives Department at The Royal Air Force Museum Hendon which holds records on wartime crashes have also been quite helpful in supplying me with written extracts - from the Form 1180 Accident Card for PB 304. The Ministry of Defence Legal Department prohibits the facsimile copying of the cards and only written extracts can be supplied but even the brief details contained on the Form 1180 give a further insight into the accident and what the Air Staff thought had caused it.

> AOC and AOC in C concur: aircraft was out of
> control. Pilot probably lost control in cloud
> and did not regain it due to bad visibility.
> Bombs exploded in crash, aircraft burnt out on
> crashing. It is possible that aircraft was hit
> unbeknown to the pilot and this had
> a bearing on the accident.

This extract from the Form 1180 is the second official account to suggest that PB 304 might have been damaged by enemy action, the other one being The Parliamentary Journal, Hansard, for August 1944.

The details of the report on the crash were written on RAF Form 765 (C): a document completed in the event of flying accidents or forced landings, "Not Attributable To Enemy Action". The fact that it was filed on this form provides us with the first contradiction concerning official statements, . Bureaucracy in RAF administration dictated that the Form 765 had to be submitted not later than four days after an accident occurred. Four days after the crash at Salford rescue teams were still working on the crash site but paperwork had to be completed. In the circumstances and because of a lack of information, for clerical convenience the Form 765 may have seemed more appropriate.

The report on the accident involving PB 304 contains technical details of the aircraft and brief remarks from the squadron commander and station commander. Section 11 of the Form 765 requested information from an appropriate specialist officer. A Squadron Leader Taylor completed this section and wrote only, "Accident being investigated by AIB". The comments of 106 Squadron's Commanding Officer, Wing Commander Piercy, are recorded below.

Aircraft apparently flew into river bank adjoining built-up area in daylight. Low cloud was prevailing at the time. The aircraft returning from an abortive operation and was carrying a full bomb-load. Pilot was experienced. Until the results of the investigation are available it is useless to hazard any theories or recommendations.

Group Captain McKechne the Station Commander, was a little more imaginative and his comments suggest several possible causes.

1. It is doubtful if any investigation will be able to find the answer to the accident. Either of the following may have caused the accident.

(1) Pilot was in difficulties due to some engine trouble and had to descend.

(2) Pilot broke cloud on track from Squires Gate to base before he should have done.

2. With regards to 1 (2) both the pilot and navigator were experienced in their duties.

When an aircraft was involved in an accident there were two ways that its circumstances would normally be investigated. A Court of Inquiry could be set up or an official Investigation carried out. The Court of Inquiry comprised of a President and a Board of Officers who considered the evidence presented before them. An Investigation was normally carried out by a single officer who held the rank of Flight Lieutenant or above but both the proceedings of the Court of Inquiry and Investigation were presented on RAF Form 412. This form contained the names of witnesses; an account of the incident; a detailed history of the pilot's experience. In section 10 of the Form 412 were written the conclusions - followed by the remarks of the group commander and if necessary, Bomber Command's Commander-in-Chief, Air Chief Marshal Arthur Harris.

A report written on a Form 412 came into my possession about another accident concerning a Halifax bomber that crashed at Blackley near Manchester in October 1944. It contains a detailed list of nine witnesses including several civilians and overall is much more detailed than a Form 765, stretching to five large pages. According to information from some official sources an Investigation was carried out into the crash involving PB 304, although nobody can provide me with details of it because of the Official Secrets Act. The Canadian Archive's Office in Ottawa who supplied me with the Form 765 for PB 304 and Form 412 for JN 886, claim that no Form 412 exists for PB 304. Canadian Archives hold copies of all documents concerning Canadian aircrew and accidents to aircraft with Canadian personnel on board.

The fact that the Canadian Archives Office does not have an Investigation report clearly suggests that none was ever made and the issue of whether or not an Investigation took place, is important in the context of how the RAF viewed the loss of the Lancaster and what action was taken. Although several sources state that PB 304 might have crashed as a result of enemy action in the end the paperwork was processed as for an aircraft whose loss was not attributable to enemy action. That is another contradiction and probably means no investigation of any sort was carried out.

A letter sent from the Royal Canadian Air Force Overseas Headquarters Casualty Branch in Oxford Street, London, to the Secretary in the Department of National Defence for Air, states that no Investigation was carried out and gives the reasons. It was sent via The Secretary for The National League for Defence and reads as follows:

Although Form 765 stated "accident being investigated by AIB", AIB investigation was not made. It would appear that the nature of the wreckage and extent of the damage resulting from the explosion of the full bomb load made any further investigations impossible. Letter dated 22 October, 1944, from the Commanding Officer of No 106 Squadron to Mr Reid stated that no further details of the accident had been forthcoming and it was highly unlikely that the cause of the crash could now be discovered.

This letter is dated 2 August, 1945, and the Commanding Officer who sent the letter referred to in the correspondence in October 1944 would have been Wing Commander Stevens, who had taken over command of 106 Squadron. This letter affords the clearest indication that no AIB Investigation was made. The same communication refers to Mrs Jeannie Reid's request for information about her son's duties at Bomber Command HQ at High Wycombe in late 1943, as she and other close relatives were keen to find out as much as possible about the circumstances surrounding the loss of their loved ones.

In his letter to the parents of Sergeant Barnes dated 3 August, 1944, Wing Commander Piercy said that something very serious and out-of-the-ordinary must have happened. He praised the skill of Flight Lieutenant Lines and his crew saying, "That some serious trouble had developed seems certain for your son's pilot had such skill and experience that he would have extricated himself from normal difficulties". This is a wonderful endorsement of Peter Lines's ability as a pilot by his CO and worthy recognition of the situation in which he and his crew found themselves. A similar letter was sent to the families of all members of the crew on the same date and the wing commander told them the aircraft was attempting a forced landing.

Several years ago the aviation historian Ron Collier was looking through records at The Ministry of Defence. During his search he came across a reference to PB 304 and information that makes the mystery of what happened even more puzzling. Many of the details did not match the facts and the time of the crash is recorded as 0300 hours when we know it happened shortly after 1000. The date is correct but the type of flight is noted as being a "cross-country". This might be an excusable error because few people would gather from its route that PB 304 was returning from operations. All the other details concerning the name of the pilot and airframe are correct.

The report claims that the port mainframe caught fire and the aircraft went out of control. The cause of the accident is given as "leaking fuel tanks coupled with bad wing ventilation". After the Canadian letter stating that no Investigation was carried out, the source of this information is so much more confusing but cannot be ignored. How could anyone establish from small fragments of aeroplane what caused it to crash?

This question brings me back to Mr Petherick's statement in The House of Commons. He said that the Chancellor should be made aware that the aircraft was "struggling home as a result of enemy action". For him to have said such a thing without access to information supporting his claim, would have made him look foolish in the eyes of the Chancellor. Also the speed that Mr Cary's demands were agreed to after initial resistance to claims for compensation makes me suspect other factors were at work. Did the authorities know something which they were - and still are unwilling to release to the general public?

It was almost impossible for any such evidence to have been found in the wreckage of PB 304. The only other possible source might have originated with a last minute message transmitted or broadcast by the Lancaster's wireless operator, Sergeant Arthur Young. Such a message could have been sent over the emergency frequency of 303 kHz on the Long Wave band. Three signals about the incident were transmitted from Ringway on 31 July to The Air Ministry notifying it of events.

Access to and copies of T578, T584 and T588 are not available so their contents remain a mystery as well as the reason for them being sent from Ringway. Ringway played a part in the tragedy - but what was its role? Did Sergeant Young or Flight Lieutenant Lines make contact with flying control at Ringway and tell them of their difficulties? Had Peter Lines set course for the airfield which was the home of 1 Parachute Training centre when he realized his crippled aircraft could not make it? The answers to these questions will never be known but if

121

we ask another question, might we not be nearer the truth - If a pilot of a heavy bomber experienced the kind of problems faced by Flight Lieutenant Lines - on recovery would he not set course for and request permission to land at the nearest sizable airfield?

PB 304 was one of five Lancasters which failed to return on 30 July and two Halifaxes also crashed on their return to England. NE 121 of 97 Squadron crashed on fire approximately 15 kilometres south-east of St Lô and of the nine men on board, only three managed to escape alive. One of those was Pilot Officer Moore, who reported that the port inner engine of NE 121 had caught fire and Flight Lieutenant Baker gave the order to abandon the aircraft. Moore was first out, after it had already hit the ground and exploded, at which juncture the Germans took him prisoner and later told him that with the exceptions of Squadron Leader Stevens and Warrant Officer Hunter, the rest of the crew were dead. The Lancaster had been hit by flak on two separate occasions.

3 Group suffered the heaviest losses with 75, 115 and 514 Squadrons all losing a single Lancaster. Several former airmen have described the scene over the target area that Sunday morning and talk of a concentrated flak barrage. As well as the flak and as was to be expected in the crowded sky, there was a collison between a Halifax and a Lancaster from 75 Squadron. Sergeant Nairn's Lancaster, HK 558 D for Dog, dived into the ground and its seven crew were all killed. The other Lancasters lost were PB 130 from 115 Squadron and LL 733 of 514 Squadron. All fourteen airmen aboard these two aircraft also died.

The Halifax, N for Nuts, which collided with Sergeant Nairn's Lancaster was from 420 Squadron in 6 Group and it was able to fly on to make an emergency landing at White Waltham near Maidenhead. At 0920 hours the aircraft touched down, only to run off the end of the runway and onto the GWR railway line, blocking the track, the pilot having unfortunately made his approach on the short runway, which was not big enough for a four-engined bomber. The crew of N for Nuts had aborted the operation very early on so it too had its bombs on board and after the initial impact the Halifax caught fire, one member of its crew being killed when the bombs exploded. Of the eight man crew, five were seriously wounded and two received slight injuries. This Halifax was one of only two aircraft from 6 Group to abort.

Another Halifax crashed near Moreton-in-the-Marsh when LL 545 of 102 Squadron tried to make what must have been an emergency landing at Enstone, a satellite of Moreton, situated to its south-east.

For some reason flying control at Enstone would not accept the aircraft and its pilot was told to return to the main airfield. Something went wrong and the Halifax crashed into trees near Blockley killing Flight Sergeant Hulme and his crew. Enstone happens to be only a short distance away from Pershore and the crew's problems also seemed to have begun along the route home - and like those on board the Lancaster at Salford - the Halifax ran out of sky.

In view of what happened to other aircraft it is most likely that PB 304 was damaged by enemy action caused by light flak or machine-gun bullets. If eye-witness accounts are to be believed a fire had broken out on board the Lancaster as a result of the loss of coolant and one or both of the port engines had ceased to function - or were in the final stages of providing the Lancaster with any power for propulsion. The claim that the fire resulted from leaking fuel tanks can not be totally dismissed although little remained of the wreckage - indeed hardly enough to come to the conclusion that a failing fuel system caused the crash. Only one explanation might reasonably suggest that the aircraft had fuel problems and that is if the Lancaster had a history of such trouble. As far as we know it did not but the technical logs that could confirm this are no longer available.

At least one other major factor indirectly affected the fate of the seven airmen on board PB 304 as well as those on other aircraft which crashed. The weather played a major part in the day's events, both over the target area and at home in England for the return of the bombers. An examination of the forecast supplied to the Chiefs of Staff at 0430 hours is set out below and the summary of actual conditions show how far out the forecast was.

FORECAST SUPPLIED TO CHIEFS OF STAFF
AT 0430 HOURS

For take-off 6, 4, 1, and 5 Groups will have 10/10ths cloud, base between 200 and 500 ft above surface and visibility 1-2 miles. The top of cloud about 2,000 ft with nothing above, but in a narrow area near the coast and in 6 Group, layers of cloud are expected above the very low cloud, and some local rain. 3 and 8 Groups should have no cloud below 1,500 ft and moderate visibility.

For return, cloud in northern groups is not expected to have lifted above 600 ft by 1000 hours, but by 1100 hours improvement to over 1,000 ft with large increasing breaks should be general. During the morning cloud in 3 and 8 Groups should remain above 1,500 ft and be well broken, and visibility moderate. 92 and 91 Groups, and east of 91

Group will have fog by 0600 hours, or very soon afterwards, a rapid improvement is expected in 91 and 92 Groups. The west of 93 Group should have workable conditions and reliable diversions are expected in the American stations south of $52\frac{1}{2}$ degrees north and at stations on or near the south coast from Exeter eastwards; also in SW Wales.

TARGET: Good prospects of 5/10ths or less Cu.cloud, base between 2,000 ft, tops 5,000 ft,with slight risk of patches of cloud at about 1,000 ft.

SUMMARY OF ACTUAL CONDITIONS

CAEN AREA (Target) 10/10ths cloud SC from French coast to target area, base 2,000 ft - 2,500 ft, tops 5,000 ft - 6,000 ft. Wind at 7,000 ft 306 degrees 26 mph.

ROUTE 9/10ths SC in two layers, lower tops 5 - 6,000 ft, upper layer between 7,000 and 10,000 ft; occasional Cu tops to 12,000 ft. Cloud became well broken over the Channel, but reforming over enemy coast.

The most obvious difference between the forecast conditions and those actually experienced, concerns the amount of cloud found above the target area. 5/10ths or less was forecast but a complete blanket of cloud covered Normandy right down to and below 2,000 ft. By the time the Chiefs-of-Staff examined the weather conditions the crews had been briefed and were preparing for take-off. Presumably the Air Staff were aware of the bad conditions but it was too late to cancel the operation and a commitment to support the army, albeit reluctantly meant it had to go ahead.

The ultimate effect of the weather was to delay aircraft loaded with bombs from landing at their bases and forcing pilots to carry out long cross-country flights. For most of the morning airfields in Lincolnshire and Yorkshire were covered in low cloud, below 1,000 ft and nearly 200 bombers landed at Woodbridge, including 12 from 115 Squadron, while others diverted to Manston. The lessons of "Black Thursday" on 16 December, 1943, had again been ignored and aircraft were dispatched when weather conditions in England were known to be unfit for their return. On that day in 1943 when 30 aircraft crashed because there was nowhere for them to land, the Indian gunner's crew had successfully battled through the atrocious weather, as he had on many occasions since and was by now the finished and experienced product. Just once was he denied that essential attribute of the wartime flier - a little luck.

Of those aircraft which did bomb the targets, many of the crews went down so dangerously low as to cause them to be considerably damaged by the effects of blast from their own bombs. The aircraft had been bombed up and refuelled during the night and to change the fuses on the bombs, would have caused considerable delay and inconvenience but increased the safety factor. In the end and as Air Vice-Marshal Bennet complained about army co-operation operations, their planning was a matter of bureaucracy and nothing could be changed despite the fact that arrangements had often been made hours earlier they did not allow for any flexibility.

No single factor or error can be blamed for the loss of Peter Lines and his crew. Bad planning and the weather bear an apportionment of responsibility but in the end it was a technical problem that caused the Lancaster to crash because it no longer had the power to remain in the air. It had been damaged by enemy action only five days earlier when it was hit near the rear turret while flying over the French coast but that should have had no bearing on the accident. From the results of my research and investigations I have formed the opinion that the Lancaster was damaged over Normandy and crashed after a failure of its engine cooling systems.

Regardless of anyone's conclusions, factors that contributed to the airmen's deaths should be separated from the causes of the crash. With that in mind the order given at briefing that morning for pilots to "return with their bomb loads" must have had a major influence on the fact that none of the Lancaster's crew got a chance to escape. Flight Lieutenant Lines was not the kind of officer to disobey orders and forfeited his own life and those of his crew while almost certainly trying to save the lives of people beneath the flight path of his aircraft.

Whatever the intentions were of Peter Lines at the beginning of the emergency, I am convinced that in the final moments he was well aware that he had little hope of making any kind of normal landing. I have walked the length and breadth of Littelton Road Playing Fields on many occasions and I am convinced that regardless of his skill or ability, which have never been in question, the best he could have hoped to achieve was a forced landing, allowing his crew to escape. Had the aircraft's port wing tip not hit Mrs Chase's house, this would very likely have happened and the seven airmen might have had some chance of getting out alive. The majority of eye-witnesses talked about a fire, but nobody can confirm whether the aircraft had its wheels down, so we can only presume that the Lancaster's undercarriage was extended - although in the final instance it failed to matter.

Had things turned out differently, then within an hour the seven airmen might have been sitting in Raymond Barnes' front room in West Drive, Swinton, drinking tea and joking about their narrow escape. It is quite possible that Flight Lieutenant Lines would have been decorated because his crew could have proclaimed his achievement. But it was not to be and seven men died, leaving a mystery which affected the lives of many people forever obscured by the clouds of time.

Chapter 8

THE AFTERMATH

On 31 July the day after the BLUECOAT Operation, the Lancasters of 106 Squadron were in action again during operations at Joigny-La-Roche and Rilly-La-Montage, when 9 aircraft were sent to each target. Amongst this strike force was the aircraft of Flight Lieutenant Reid of 617 Squadron, who had won The Victoria Cross while flying with 61 Squadron in 1943. On this day however, the gods were not disposed to smile on earlier deeds of valour and his aircraft, ME 557, was one of the two lost on the Rilly-La-Montage raid. Fortunately Reid managed to parachute to safety and spent the remainder of the war in a prisoner of war camp.

As is to be expected in any campaign the crews who flew through the Summer of 1944 suffered mixed fortunes and many would not survive to witness the end of hostilities in May 1945. On 6 August, Warrant Officer Cunningham completed his tour with a final four-and-a-half-hour flight to St Leu d'Esserant and during his 35 operations he had flown 196 hours and 45 minutes, out of a total flying time of 682 hours and 45 minutes. Six days later on 12 August, Cunningham and his crew left Metheringham for the last time and departed in a Halifax for Croft in North Yorkshire, where the seven men split up before going onto courses and commencing training duties.

Having begun their operational tour on 19 February, 1944, with a raid on Leipzig, Jim Cunningham and his crew must have wondered what the future held for them, since 78 aircraft were lost that night representing some 13% of the force. Any chance of them completing a tour must have seemed quite slim. After flying a succession of spare aircraft such as ME 669 the crew were assigned their own personal Lancaster and ND 535 became their first "Queenie". When that was lost in March with another crew, they received ND 868 and took this aircraft so much to their hearts that they hated flying in anything else.

Former sergeant air gunner Derek Whiting recalled an occasion on 30 May when their aircraft diverted to Little Horwood in Buckinghamshire because of bad weather at Metheringham. They were surprised to discover that the only spare beds were in the WAAF compound as the main camp was full; but before they were allowed in, the WAAF "G" read the riot act and gave them a lecture on what they could do and how they should behave! A short time later

127

Metheringham was fitted with FIDO and they never landed away from base again.

Jim Cunningham's crew were good friends of the fitters and riggers who looked after their aircraft, though they and most other airmen knew it did not do to become too familiar. Sergeant Rasmussen designed a picture for them which was painted on their Lancaster, beneath the pilot's window, It was a blonde nude, based on the WAAF corporal who drove the crew bus and it portrayed her reclining on a sofa naked. Beneath it were the words, "Q Up!" and above it, "Nau Clues!". The latter referred to the answer that Warrant Officer Cunningham always gave when the ground crew asked where they had been, in an exaggerated Scottish brogue, he would claim that they had got lost. The reclining nude continued to be painted onto those Lancasters with the letter "Q" and subsequently flew with Lieutenant Becker of the South African Air Force and Ken Kiesling an Australian, except that the words changed to "Sari Marais" and "Kiesling's Krazy Hunts".

The highlight of Jim Cunningham's spell on 106 Squadron came on 10 June when he and his crew formed part of a small force of Lancasters which attacked a railway line near Orleans. The award of The Distinguished Flying Cross was normally made to commissioned officers only, although a small number of senior NCOs did get the medal, rather than the DFM. After leaving 106 and undergoing an instructors' course at Silverstone, Warrant Officer Cunningham went on to 85 OTU at Husbands Bosworth, where he taught pilots to fly the Vickers Wellington and after the war ended, he was transferred to 105 OTU where he again instructed on Wellingtons at Bramcote and Nuneaton.

On 1 August, only two days after PB 304 crashed while returning with its bomb load, there was another similarly aborted operation on flying bomb storage sites during which 106 Squadron again split its force into two sending 12 Lancasters to Siracourt and five to Breteque. Altogether 5 Group contributed 153 Lancasters to a total of 777 and when they arrived at the target areas, crews found the situation was in chaos with aircraft flying above and below cloud, the base of which was approximately 6,500 ft. Crews had been briefed to bomb from between 16-18,000 ft at Siracourt and at Breteque between 10-12,000 ft, with marking again carried out by 8 Group's Oboe Mosquitos from 5,000 ft. As he had done on 30 July, the Master Bomber transmitted the Marmalade signal to abort the operation and very few crews got the chance to attack the objectives. The general opinion again seemed to be that the raid had again been called off far too late.

On this occasion 617 Squadron aircraft were carrying 12,000 lb "Tallboys" with half-hour delayed fuses, whilst other aircraft in the main force carried 11 x 1,000 lb bombs and four x 500 lb bombs. Some crews again chose to jettison their loads while others decided to return with them, including Syd Geater's skipper, Flying Officer Merideth, who took his bombs back to base - but for some reason landed fifty minutes after everyone else and the crew were just about to be listed as "Missing" when they landed at 1915 hours. This was only the crew's tenth operation and they would not complete their tour without some close shaves - so dramatically exemplified earlier when on 12 July whilst bombing marshalling yards at Culmont, when they were shadowed by a Ju 88 and only escaped because they were able to use the "Fishpond" radar set to monitor its movements! Altogether twenty nine 1,000 lb bombs were jettisoned in the North Sea and ninety seven returned to Metheringham. Forty eight 500lb bombs were also returned to the airfield.

Bombs fell into several different categories of General Purpose, Medium Capacity, High Capacity and some types fitted with American lugs. The main difference between a General Purpose bomb and one classed as Medium Capacity was the amount of explosives it contained, as a proportion of its overall weight. A GP bomb could contain as little as 30% explosives, while for an MC bomb it could be as much as 50%. The proportion of explosives in a High Capacity bomb was up to 70% of its weight. During the Summer of 1944 Medium and High Capacity bombs were in short supply and General Purpose bombs had to be used to make up numbers. 500 lb GP bombs had something of a reputation for being unreliable but there were huge stocks of them and the loss of a few hundred would not be missed. Stocks of MC and HC bombs were limited, especially 1,000 lb bombs and whenever possible it was requested that crews return them. This however does not explain the urgency of the request to 106 Squadron crews on the morning of 30 July to return their bombs. As far as is known all 106 Squadron's Lancasters carried only General Purpose bombs.

During the night of 7/8 August another army support operation took place with a massive force of 1,019 aircraft attacking five aiming points, although again only about half the force bombed the targets and the remainder either returned their bombs or jettisoned them in the North Sea. 10 Lancasters were lost on the night, including LM 641 P for Peter from 106 Squadron flown by Flying Officer Rabone and his crew on their tenth operation. The fate of the crew was mixed as two were killed, four were taken prisoner while the navigator evaded capture.

An attack on Brunswick during the night of 12/13 August nearly proved fatal for the 106 Squadron CO and his crew when Wing Commander Piercy had to nurse ND 682 K for King back to Metheringham. According to Sergeant Goodman the rear gunner, the flak extended from 400 ft right up to 19,000 ft and the Lancaster was badly damaged, severely testing Sergeant Clarke's abilities, who as the flight engineer did a great job in getting them back again. Sergeant Goodman wrote an appreciation of Clarke's actions in his log book, together with a note of his own personal contribution in shooting up a searchlight over the target area.

The Brunswick raid was something of an experiment because the Pathfinders did not take part and there was no marking of any kind since crews were supposed to find the target by using H2s alone and even with a skilled operator, accuracy was a problem. Many crews failed to find Brunswick and bombed the towns and cities around it - typified for instance by Flying Officer Merideth's crew who, bombed Hildersheim to the south-east of Brunswick and over twenty miles away from the target.

On 14 August, 106 Squadron took part in a further army support operation on seven German positions in the Falaise Gap but on this occasion something went badly wrong and bombs fell onto friendly forces. It was reported that 13 men of the 12th Canadian Field regiment were killed and many more injured. There are conflicting stories about what happened but one explanation claimed that the Canadians fired off flares to warn the bombers of their position. They fired the colour of the day, which happened to be yellow but this was also the colour of some types of Target Indicator and the flare served only to draw the attention of more bomb aimers and pilots with understandably disastrous results. Wing Commander Piercy led the Squadron on this raid which was in fact the final operation of his second tour and since the remaining six airmen still had to complete their respective tours, they were split up to fly with other crews as and when required.

After nearly a three week break including a short period in hospital, Sergeant Robert Saul returned to operations on 14 August, in the crew of Flight Lieutenant Stewart and must have been feeling extremely depressed after hearing about the loss of Flight Lieutenant Lines and his crew. According to his son John, Sergeant Saul's best friends were fellow gunner John Davenport and the Canadian navigator Flying Officer Harry Reid, who despite the fact that he was a commissioned officer, had visited the Saul household in West Haddon near Rugby on several occasions. This was Saul's seventh operation on 106 squadron and it was against shipping in Brest Harbour where the German cruisers Clemenceau and Gueydon were both damaged. Previously he had occupied the rear turret, but now he flew in the mid-upper turret of PD 214 D for Dog and replaced a Sergeant Williams.

Back in Salford the debate continued as to whether the pilot of the bomber should be awarded a medal for his actions, as originally suggested by Alderman Leonard Webb, JP. The loss of the Lancaster at Salford and the Halifax at Ryhope involved the same kind of considerations since each aircraft had suffered varying degrees of damage, and both collided with houses on the final approach as their pilots struggled with the controls searching for somewhere to land. Pilot Officer Barton had also been additionally disadvantaged by the fact that his aircraft ran out of fuel.

An extract from the official citation announcing the award of The Victoria Cross to Pilot Officer Barton best describes what he did next: "Before a suitable landing place could be found, the port engines stopped. Pilot Officer Barton therefore ordered the three remaining members of his crew to take up their crash stations. Then with only one engine working, he made a gallant attempt to land clear of the houses over which he was flying. The aircraft finally crashed and Pilot Officer Barton lost his life, but his three comrades survived". A similar account might have been written about the actions of Flight Lieutenant Lines but nobody escaped from PB 304 to tell the tale.

The type of operation on which a crew had been engaged, was of course one of the factors which could be expected to influence recommendations for the award of decorations for gallantry to individual airmen and in this respect Pilot Officer Barton's aircraft was returning from Nuremberg on the night that Bomber Command suffered its heaviest losses. There are arguments about how many aircraft were lost on this raid, but with those that crashed on their return, the true figure is probably over 100. Barton's Halifax LK 797 was hit and damaged several times, both on the way to the target and on the way home but despite some of his crew baling out Barton pressed on to the target and the courage of the young 23 year old, who carried on without his navigator, captured the imagination of the country. News of Barton's award broke on 27 June, 1944, and it is likely to have been fresh in the minds of many people at the time of the crash at Salford.

One reason that might have prevented Flight Lieutenant Lines receiving any award, even had someone survived, was specifically related to the nature of his target on July 30th. In April 1944 Bomber

Command decided that operations against targets in France were not as dangerous as those directed at Germany itself and in future would only count as "One Third" of an operation, which announcement angered many airmen who thought they were being cheated by an attempt to lengthen their tour. On the night of 3/4 May, 1944, 346 aircraft attacked German Panzer Units at Mailly-Le-Camp and 42 Lancasters were lost amounting to 11% of the force - far above the 5% magical figure that Bomber Command considered acceptable and heavier than against some targets in Germany. After Mailly-Le-Camp the policy was reversed but in the eyes of many senior officers French operations did not carry the same risk and even as late as July 1944, there was talk of getting crews to do two operations in one day and count them as one. The chances of aircrew on daylight army support operations above France being considered for such a distinguished medal as The Victoria Cross were poor.

Rather ironically Salford does have a claim to a connection with an airman who was awarded The Victoria Cross in the Second World War. Flight Sergeant Arthur Aaron received his award for bravery on the night of 12/13 August, 1943, when despite beng hit in the face by a bullet during a raid on Turin, helped the bomb aimer and flight engineer to fly and land his Stirling on an airfield in North Africa. Though he could not speak through his shattered jaw, he wrote down instructions and used sign language to pass on information. Arthur came from Leeds and attended Roundhay School but for a while lived in Salford, where he was studying architecture. After joining the local Air Training Corps Arthur became a regular member of 319 Squadron (Broughton) and left its ranks only to join the RAF. For many years a replica of Flight Sergeant Aaron's Victoria Cross hung on the wall of The Salford Royal Air Force Association Club, as a proud reminder of the connection with the past.

Some crews on 106 Squadron transferred to 83 or 97 Squadrons at Coningsby, a short distance away to the east and up to April 1944 both these squadrons had belonged to 8 Group, better known as The Pathfinders. The squadrons now formed part of 5 Group's pathfinding force and crews worked under orders from Air Vice-Marshal Cochrane in place of Air Vice-Marshal Bennett. Instead of doing 30 operations to complete a tour, aircrew on Pathfinder squadrons did 60, although crews on their second tours often only had to do an extra 25. The PFF relied upon volunteers, as were all RAF aircrew, but in this case to do an extra long tour and a job that many others would not consider doing. Although 5 Group Headquarters was always on the lookout for crews who would be willing to transfer, its efforts to maintain high standards inevitably resulted in disappointments when crews had to be rejected.

Flying Officer Vic Cuttle and his crew, under the command of Squadron Leader A.L. Williams joined 106 Squadron in April 1944, but after completing 20 operations they transferred to 83 Squadron on 2 August. During their time on 106, Squadron Leader Willliams had been the "A" Flight Commander and Flying Officer Cuttle was his wireless operator but almost as soon as they arrived at Coningsby, Vic became the Deputy Signals Leader and because of his extensive experience Squadron Leader Williams immediately took command of "B" Flight.

On the night of 25 August the crew took-off on a long flight to Darmstadt as part of a 190 strong force with Lancasters from 5 Group which failed because the Master Bomber and his deputies were lost. The aircraft departed Coningsby at 2100 hours and by 0055 hours they had just reached the turning point for the final leg to the target when suddenly a tremendous explosion rocked Squadron Leader Williams' Lancaster, followed by a second one to starboard which threw the aircraft over on its back and left the crew hanging upside down in their harnesses. At the time Vic said he felt no fear, for he had seen many Lancasters go down, although he never thought it would happen to him, but in any case in a few moments he thought his life would end very quickly.

To the surprise of everyone the Lancaster suddenly righted itself and though he was not connected to the intercom, Vic Cuttle understood frenzied hand signals to indicate the aircraft was to be abandoned. Then he saw the navigator Syd Astley rise from his seat and heard him shout, "Jump!...Jump!" He quickly snapped on his chute and followed the navigator to the emergency hatch and as the navigator went out Vic saw someone else beside him, who he thought was the flight engineer. Just as this figure jumped out, another explosion rocked the aircraft directly below the fuselage and it seemed inevitable that whoever had last abandoned the stricken plane had jumped straight into the middle of a flak burst.

When Vic Cuttle baled out only moments later, Squadron Leader Williams was still at the controls, frantically signalling for him to go, while struggling to keep the Lancaster on an even keel. Vic said it felt like ages before the parachute opened and for a few seconds at least he thought it had not worked but suddenly it jerked open and shook his body to the bone. Heading towards a patch of canopied trees he tried to get in between them and fortunately his aim was good enough to avoid being injured on landing. His parachute caught up in a tree however and all efforts to free it failed, so he left it there, thinking he had better get away before German soldiers arrived. The first thing he did involved checking his escape kit to make sure the map and button sized compass were there along with money, Horlicks tablets, a tube of condensed milk, a bar of milk chocolate and water purifying tablets.

For six days Flying Officer Cuttle evaded capture by hiding in woods and sleeping rough. He had removed all the buttons from his uniform and taken off his medal ribbon in an attempt to look something like a local. Fortunately he never wore flying boots and his shoes looked quite ordinary which allowed him to do plenty of walking but almost proved his undoing when during one of his darkest hours he wandered into a slave labour camp and got out again only when he pretended to be a farm worker and talked gibberish to confuse the guard. Shortly afterwards, while hiding in some trees he heard a shot ring out and thought it had been fired at him but when he observed the guards he noticed they still had their rifles slung over their shoulders, which encouraged him to move on again and eventually make his way to the main road.

On 2 September Vic Cuttle arrived in Heidelberg and started to walk alongside the autobahn, hiding in hedges and bushes whenever the need arose but on reaching Mannheim felt so tired that on discovering a house with no one in it decided to take a chance. The door was open so he walked in and soon fell asleep on a sofa. When he awoke he was confronted by a group of people which unfortunately included a Luftwaffe Lieutenant from a nearby flak battery! Flying Officer Cuttle was taken prisoner to spend the remainder of the war in a POW camp and reflecting upon it later he realized he had been captured on 3 September - exactly five years to the day since war had broken out. He later found out that of the six other crew members, three had been killed in the crash including his pilot, Squadron Leader Williams. Vic would acknowledge many times during the more introspective moments of his later life, that although he had a rough time of it for a while, he at least had survived where others less fortunate had not.

On the night of 29/30 August, two other crews ran out of luck including that of the Station Commander, Group Captain McKechnie, who like his counterpart at Coningsby, Group Captain Evans-Evans, liked taking crews on their first operational flight to give them the benefit of his experience. On this occasion he was with a Sergeant Clark and his crew in JB 593 T for Tommy, taking part in an operation at Königsberg, a city which is 400 miles north-east of Berlin at the extreme limit of the Lancaster's range and well defended by night-fighters of the Luftwaffe. Only 189 Lancasters from 5 Group took part in the raid which was led by Master Bomber, Wing Commander Woodroffe, and 15 aircraft were lost. 106 Squadron lost two aircraft on the night and Flying Officer Boivin's Lancaster, ND 331 G for George, also failed to return.

Group Captain McKechnie was a popular figure at Metheringham and several crews had flown with him when their own pilots were not available, although few knew he was a holder of The George Cross, won for an act of bravery many years before at Cranwell, by dragging a pilot from his blazing aircraft. He often stepped in if a pilot went sick and former sergeant gunner Derek Whiting remembered that on 18 July he flew with him, when Warrant Officer Cunningham had a bad head cold. The next day the group captain was airborne again with Wing Commander Piercy's crew on a flying exercise but in the end his own enthusiasm for flying was his downfall and Group Captain McKechnie failed to return from what amounted to his seventh second dickie trip. No trace of JB 593 or its crew was ever found and considering the distance involved to Königsberg, the possibilities of what befell them are infinite. T for Tommy might have crashed into the sea, blown up in the air or crashed in the vast expanse of the former Soviet Union.

Although Wing Commander Piercy had just finished his second tour, he stayed on at Metheringham in command of the station on a temporary basis until Group Captain Heath arrived on 5 September to take over as permanent Station Commander. He had been posted in from 10 Air Gunnery School on Walney Island, off the coast of Barrow and the new Station Commander must have found Metheringham a large and fascinating place, after the small training station with its Martinets and Ansons. Wing Commander Piercy had already handed over his command of 106 Squadron to Wing Commander Stevens, DFC.

Lancaster ND 333 became the next S for Sugar to replace PB 304 and arrived on the squadron in September. The aircraft was second-hand and it had been delivered to 83 Squadron at Coningsby in January 1944 having completed many successful operations including several trips to Berlin. The ground crews may well have been happy that it was not new because Laurie Rasmussen claimed that some Lancasters fresh off the production line, had more than their share of teething problems including at least two which never saw operational service. One of these turned out to be infested by rats or mice which chewed through wires and cables and as quickly as the aircraft was repaired, again targeted by the vermin until eventually it became simply a source of spares. Another Lancaster was struck by lightning and despite many attempts to degauss it the bomber's compass, navigation equipment and radio remained affected by electro-magnetic forces; the entire aircraft being ultimately cannibalized and reduced to spares. ND 333 was blessed with good luck and it survived through to the end of the war.

Each airman on 106 Squadron, as throughout the whole of Bomber Command, had to find his own way of coping with the strains of operational flying and the impending possibility of an early death. Drinking was the most obvious and common pastime and many crews tended to go out together on their social excursions although by contrast much courting went on between airmen and WAAFs. A contest involving the WAAF authorities and inventive young airmen was constantly in evidence, as the latter battled to gain illicit entry into the WAAFerry. By the time one method of getting into the accommodation block was discovered however another plan had already been hatched or even put into use.

Former Sergeant wireless operator Bob Howie claimed his tour was very uneventful and his aircraft, PB 296 X for X-ray, was never attacked by fighters nor was it hit by flak. His crew which originally consisted of six senior NCOs, lived, ate and drank together, which tended to preclude their association with other crews and Bob's pilot, Flight Sergeant Archer, was later commissioned; his crew having one of the best bombing records on 106 Squadron. Although each experience was different, my research suggests that Bob's was the exception rather than the norm and the majority of crews had at least one near miss with death during their tour. There were indeed those who had several.

Flight Lieutenant Merideth and his crew led a charmed life and survived several incidents that might have ended in sudden death. On 12 July while returning from Culmont they were attacked and shadowed by a Ju 88. On 2 August PB 248 was hit and damaged by flak as they returned from Trossy and was hit again the following day, putting the port outer engine out of action. On another occasion while preparing the aircraft for take-off on a daylight raid to Deelen, Sergeant Geater the wireless operator and Flying Officer Neal the navigator heard a noise outside. Sergeant Geater saw Flying Officer Merideth stick his head outside the window to see what had happened, but decided to check it out himself and had barely climbed across the main spar when he felt someone push him from behind - the navigator in his hurry to get out. Sergeant Geater knew something had happened so quickly followed and discovered that a 1,000 lb bomb had fallen off the aircraft! Unfortunately Sergeant Bruce had been standing under the open bomb bay and as it fell the bomb tore part of his ear. After ensuring that Bruce had suffered only a minor setback and that the bomb would not explode, they called for it to be inspected by an armourer who chaffed that he would only reset the weapon if they promised not to bring it back again! No doubt a few forthright observations were exchanged while the bomb was winched on board again, and after a short delay PB 248 finally took-off.

One reason Flying Officer Merideth's crew survived was because of a team spirit that was strengthened by both work and play, in addition to which the crew also had a very good feeling about Lancaster E for Easy and believed that if they stayed with it, the aircraft would always bring them back safely. After being allocated the aircraft by the then "A" Flight Commander, Squadron Leader A.L. Williams, it took them on every operation except one: notably Chatellerault on the night of 9/10 August. On that occasion they flew in ND 331 and whilst other pilots laid claim to PB 248, including Flight Lieutenant Stewart, they argued to keep her and won. Like Q for Queenie with Jim Cunningham's crew, PB 248 similarly had a painting on its nose - not a nude this time but a large raised single finger clearly expressing the crew's opinion of authority.

Towards the end of their tour Flight Lieutenant Merideth's crew had two more narrow escapes: the first during the night of 11/12 September while on an operation to Darmstadt, when PB 248 was again shadowed by a fighter. Sergeant Geater monitoring the Fishpond radar set observed a blip closing in on them and notified his skipper that he thought it was a fighter. His observation paid off when a few minutes later the pilot of the fighter made his move, only to be confronted by gunners who were ready for him and so did not return. The crew's final stroke of good fortune occurred on the night of 23/24 September on an operation above the Dortmund-Ems Canal near Munster, when they were attacked by a fighter again. This was their last trip and 106 Squadron flew as part of a 136 strong force from the various units of 5 Group, including 617 Squadron. Some aircraft carried 12,000 lb Tallboys which could penetrate the ground to create a powerful blast effect and the canal was another well defended target. On this occasion nobody spotted the fighter until it attacked and PB 248 sustained a certain amount of damage but fortunately both aircraft and crew returned safely to Metheringham. A total of 14 Lancasters were lost on this raid.

The following morning with the airmen still fresh from lengthy celebrations, they were called over to the AOC's office to be interviewed by Air Vice-Marshal Cochrane. The AOC formally congratulated them on completing their tour and said he was glad to hear they had volunteered to continue operations with the PFF. This statement produced looks of astonishment all round as it was the first time any of them had heard about it! In the event however a potentially embarrassing situation was tactfully avoided by explaining that there must have been some kind of administrative mistake, since none of them had voiced their intention of taking on another 25 operations. After a muffled conversation between the AOC and another officer the men were quickly shuffled out of the office and nobody mentioned the PFF again. A little while later one or two of the others said they would not have minded continuing and Syd said he was not sure whether someone had mentioned that they might like to go to Coningsby or if the authorities were just trying it on. The faith his crew put in PB 248 was justified because the aircraft survived the war and from 106 Squadron it went on to serve with 115 Squadron and 5 LFS before finally being scrapped in May 1947.

Stan Goodman finished his tour before Flight Lieutenant Merideth's crew and after being obliged to fly in the mid-upper turret at the end of June, he finally got back into the rear turret for a couple of operations in August. From then on he flew in both positions and following Wing Commander Piercy's departure, did two operations with Flight Lieutenant Stewart's crew during which time he must have flown with Sergeant Saul who occupied the rear turret in the crew. Stan did not remember him because by this stage of his tour the operations had become just numbers to count towards the final tally and he hardly got to know any airmen in the crews with whom he flew. To finish off Sergeant Goodman did two operations with Flying Officer Netherwood and three with Flying Officer Ford.

On 11 September and while serving with Flying Officer Ford in PB 191 H for Harry to Darmstadt, Stan flew as rear gunner and claimed an Me 109 shot down as a "probable" followed by a trip to Stuttgart, before ending his tour on 17 September with a raid on Boulogne, as part of an army support operation involving nearly 800 aircraft. Ironically this was in his favourite aircraft ND 682 K for King, and the one he had started on six months earlier, though unhappily not all his old crew had been so fortunate and Sergeant Clarke, the flight engineer, and Sergeant Cridge, the wireless operator, were killed after being split up from Wing Commander Piercy's team.

Probably because Group Captain McKechnie was killed, former Sergeant Goodman, along with the rest of his crew, never received the awards that they had been recommended for by Wing Commander Piercy. He had put the senior NCO's forward for the DFM and the officers for the DFC after they had struggled to get back from Brunswick on 13 August. They all knew the paperwork had been completed and it had reached McKechnie's desk, but when he was killed the system broke down and it was never processed. With Wing Commander Piercy gone and Group Captain McKechnie dead, there seemed very little anyone could do about it.

In mid-September Sergeant Saul went on what proved to be his last operation with 106 Squadron, as a member of Flight Lieutenant Stewart's crew with whom he had flown regularly since August. His final missions with this crew were to Darmstadt on 11 September and again on the next night to Stuttgart. There are suggestions that he continued flying at a later date but these are the last occasions when his name appears in the squadron records and it is thought that he was taken off flying either because of illness or re-occurrence of the problems associated with his wounds. Sergeant Saul was replaced in the Stewart's crew by a Sergeant F.V. Loudenin who had flown regularly with Sergeant Bumford's crew and he started flying operations with Stewart on 18 September.

Flight Lieutenant Stewart's crew were lost on the night of 6 October during an operation on Bremen when his aircraft, PD 214, was one of five Lancasters that failed to return. For Sergeant Saul, it was probably at this point that any intentions of returning to operations with 106 Squadron, turned sour. He had lost his second crew and regardless of his own emotions and feelings, he would be subjected to the suspicious attitudes of others. It was very easy to get the reputation of being a "Jinx" and although other airmen might not have said anything to Sergeant Saul directly, many would not have wanted to be in the same crew. There is a vague possibility that he was posted to one of the PFF Squadrons at Coningsby, but again his name is not to be found in the records. He was not a young man and in this final phase may have been restricted to instructing or other ground duties as a deserved retirement from the thrust of combat.

On 5 October, 1944, just over two months after the disaster at Salford, another bomber crashed in the same area as PB 304 only on this occasion it was a Halifax. JN 886 had taken-off from Wombleton near Kirbymoorside in North Yorkshire at 1900 hours, on a night cross-country which included a flashlight exercise above Bristol. While over Bristol the starboard inner engine failed just as the aircraft had reached 18,000 ft and the young Canadian pilot, Flying Officer Cooke, attempted to feather the propeller. Finding that it would go no further than the windmilling stage, he then set course for base, having put the Halifax into a steady descent and levelled off at 10,000 ft.

The navigator gave the pilot some Gee fixes and told him to slowly descend, but base could not be located and by now the aircraft was at 1,500 ft flying various courses in an attempt to find Wombleton. They met the west coast near Blackpool and set course for base again with the navigator trying to get another Gee fix, but ended up somewhere near Manchester when the starboard outer failed. Flying Officer Cooke attempted to feather it but like the starboard inner, it would only go to the windmilling stage and it became impossible to keep the bomber in the air. At 900 ft he ordered the crew to abandon the aircraft and although the navigator, rear gunner and wireless operator baled out immediately, their parachutes hardly had time to open, so that inevitably they were badly injured on impact with the ground. The Halifax flew low above Heaton Park and its final moments were witnessed by several officers and airmen at the Aircrew Dispatch Centre, including a Squadron Leader Purdy.

At 0005 hours the Halifax crashed 50 yards south of St.Andrew's Churchyard, on Crab Lane in Blackley, approximately two-and-a- half-miles from the crash site of PB 304. An investigation was held into the crash and the engine trouble was found to have been caused by a glycol leak but eleven other reasons were also listed as being contributory factors in causing the Halifax to crash. Amongst these it should be noted that Flying Officer Cooke had previously been enabled to perform only 6 hours solo night-flying on Halifaxes and another 2 hours on dual control, in the company of an instructor. His total flying hours were 203.

The young Canadian was in effect blamed for the accident and no consideration was given to the state of his "clapped-out" aircraft. It had been delivered to 158 Squadron in September 1943 and had already been subject to an extensive operational life, before being passed over to 1666 Heavy Conversion Unit. The Halifax Mark II with its ageing Merlin XX engines had many hours recorded on its engines and airframe and, was urgently in need of a major overhaul. Ironically the Halifax's young pilot almost certainly followed the same Gee lattice line to Manchester from the coast near Blackpool as PB 304 four months earlier and fate led the two aircraft to crashing just a few miles apart.

Over on 61 Squadron at Skellingthorpe Sergeant Leonard Whitehead, former collegue of Sergeant Singh, progressed steadily through his tour. To start with he flew with a Flying Officer Fitch or a Sergeant Martin. When Martin's crew failed to return from Berlin on 21 January, 1944, he continued with Flying Officer Fitch until his crew completed their tour.

During April and while in the crew of a Flying Officer Aukland he flew in the unusual position of mid-under gunner - a somewhat euphemistic term applied to the operators of a heavy calibre machine-gun. It was trained through a hole cut in the floor, where the H2s radar was housed and was quite logically conceived as a sizable deterrent to any fighters which might try to sneak up underneath a bomber. However the gunner had to stand all the time and remained strapped in a harness, to prevent him falling through the hole! Moreover it is not clear whether Bomber Command was aware at this time that German fighters, were equipped with Schräge Musik, the upward firing cannon that had such a deadly effect. Nevertheless the Air Chiefs-of-Staff knew of the threat the fighters posed beneath the bombers and the mid-under gunner was there to stop them. Sergeant Whitehead was accordingly required to make four trips in this position.

On 1 May his aircraft was badly shot up over Toulouse and the bomb aimer died in Sergeant Whitehead's arms on the way home. Flying Officer Aukland received an immediate DFC, and the flight engineer a DFM. The air gunner completed his tour on 7 July after taking part in 35 operations, including seven trips to Berlin and Sergeant Whitehead also flew on the Nuremberg operation when Bomber Command suffered its heaviest losses. After finishing operational flying he was posted to 1660 Heavy Conversion Unit at Swinderby as an instructor.

Flight Lieutenant John Stratford, friend and former colleague of Peter Lines, joined 166 Squadron from Number 1 Lancaster Finishing School on 13 July, 1944. Initially he and his crew undertook a couple of cross-country exercises and on 17 July John performed his 'second dickie' trip on flying bomb sites with a Flying Officer Singleton, who only a short time afterwards along with his crew, failed to return. On 25 July Flight Lieutenant Stratford flew on his first operation to Stuttgart and two nights later on the 28th they visited Stuttgart again but this time the nature of the excursion - their second operation - was to remain long in their minds. John said nothing happened but it was a most uncomfortable flight, especially on the long run-in to the target, when all the flares dropped by night-fighters illuminated the sky just like daylight. Although he did not know it at the time, only a short distance away that night was his old friend Peter Lines, experiencing his first, and as it tragically proved, his final operation above a German city.

Throughout their tour Flight Lieutenant Stratford's crew flew in various Lancasters but his regular aircraft was V for Victor and both he and his crew tried to think positively to the exclusion of superstitious practices or the carrying of mascots. When they had completed over 25 operations, John would talk to his crew before take-off and he would remind them, that though the end was in sight, they should not become complacent. On one occasion after he had spoken a few words, the rear gunner called over the intercom, "Our Second Skipper!" This served to remind the crew of their worst experience over Stuttgart on 28 July.

On 9 November, 1944, John's crew finished their tour in a wholly exceptional way with an aborted operation. The target was Wanne-Eickel in Germany, but as they were attaining height on the outbound leg his Lancaster developed engine trouble and John had to shut the faulty motor down. He spoke to the crew, which included two screened instructors, as some of his team had already completed their tour and John told them that they could neither make the height nor keep up with the rest of the force. He asked for their opinion and they agreed it would be best to return although fully aware that often an abortive trip would not count towards their tour. After some discussion about the circumstances of his early return however the Flight Commander decreed it should count and as it was also his wife's birthday, John concluded his operational tour a very happy man.

One man who did not survive to the end of his tour was the wireless operator in John's crew. Flying Officer Buckland had from the beginning been troubled with a carbuncle which had prevented him from flying and had caused him to miss eleven operations. Amongst those wireless operators who were put into the crew to replace him, was a young unknown actor called Donald Pleasance who flew with Flight Lieutenant Stratford on just a single occasion. Flying Officer Buckland was left to fly his outstanding operations with other crews and suffered the final irony on his last mission when his aircraft went missing - never to be sighted again. John felt particularly upset because like Peter Lines, he had know Buckland from the days when they both lived in Ealing. For the sake of a carbuncle Flying Officer Buckland had lost his life and the perils of unforeseen circumstances when flying with more than one crew had again been highlighted in the gravest and most dramatic of ways.

John eventually got around to writing to Peter Lines and the letter was answered by his father, who informed him of the tragedy at Salford. Mr Lines claimed in his correspondence that the RAF had been negligent and were responsible for his son's death, especially in connection with what proved to be a critical decision in ordering Peter to return with his bomb load. It is not known whether Mr Lines had been subject to military service or understood the workings of the military, but he understandably felt aggrieved at the manner of losing his eldest son for what were seemingly questionable reasons. From examining the records sent to me by Canadian Archives I know that the Reid family in Toronto felt similiarly frustrated, having received little information and what proved to be only false promises of a full investigation.

In May 1945 Warrant Officer Cunningham was posted from 62 OTU at Ousten, to 105 OTU at Bramcote and throughout July he instructed on Wellingtons, doing circuits, landings, flap-less landings and dual checks. On 2 August, almost exactly a year after leaving 106 Squadron, he had an accident in which he was very badly injured. The day's sortie involved a five hour cross- country flight, in S for Sugar, with a Flight Lieutenant Horry, via Lincoln to the North Sea before landing at Ousten. Having taken-off again they flew via Bradford back to Bramcote but either because an engine failed or Flight Lieutenant Horry was attempting an asymmetric landing, the Wellington crashed.

Jim Cunningham suffered spinal injuries and was taken to the EMS Hospital at Warwick, where he remained until 15 February, 1946, being subsequently admitted to the RAF Hospital Hartbury where he remained in care until 3 April. It is not known how badly the other crew members were injured, but Jim noted in his log that the wireless operator was bruised and in a state of shock, while the navigator received only slight injuries. Warrant Officer Cunningham did not fly again until 10 July, when he was posted to 1381 TCU at Desborough. He was demobilized on 18 September, 1946, though he continued to fly in the Volunteer Reserve for many years and later flew Chipmunks at number 12 Air Experience Flight near Edinburgh.

106 Squadron flew its last operational mission on the night of 25/26 April, 1945, when 14 Lancasters bombed oil refineries at Tonsberg in Norway. The last Lancaster of the war was lost on this raid though its crew, from 463 Squadron survived. During May the Squadron helped to repatriate prisoners from France and over 400 POWs were flown home. Wing Commander Stevens remained as the 106 Squadron CO until February 1945 but his predecessor, Wing Commander Piercy, was killed in 1946 while flying a Proctor in Iraq. His aircraft is thought to

have crashed into the River Euphrates during a sand storm.

106 Squadron was finally disbanded on 18 February, 1946. Airmen in its ranks had won a total of 267 decorations and a Victoria Cross awarded to Sergeant Norman Jackson.

Chapter 9

OF FAMILY, FRIENDS AND COLLEAGUES

Sergeant Robert Saul came from Bamber Bridge on the outskirts of Preston in Lancashire where in his civilian trade he was an armature winder working for English Electric and British Thompson Houston. After Robert was married his first child, a son, was born in Bamber Bridge on 31 May, 1934, and the family moved to West Haddon near Rugby in 1939. Having been born in 1909, by the time he joined the RAF in August 1942, he was already 35 years old and with 106 Squadron in July 1944 he was the oldest member of PB 304's crew - probably one of the oldest airmen flying on the squadron with the exception of senior officers, like Group Captain McKechnie.

The other gunner, Sergeant Davenport was 31 years old and as he also lived in the Midlands the two men had something in common, as well as the fact that they were both married. Robert Saul's son John, remembered his father coming home on leave and talking about his friend "Tubby" Davenport and Harry, the friendly Canadian, who liked to visit his father's home. It was a common and real enough fear amongst airmen, that once they were separated from other members of their crew, any collective security they had disappeared. Together the seven men were a team and shared their fate as one. If airmen were split up, as unfortunately happened to Sergeant Saul, the chances of each airman completing his tour safely, diminished proportionally. Having suffered the loss of a first crew, Robert Saul was extremely lucky to survive a second time, and must have reflected on his singular good fortune many times during the remainder of his life.

Sometime after leaving 106 Squadron Sergeant Saul was promoted to Flight Sergeant and he remained in the RAF until March 1945 when he resumed his civilian job as an armature winder. The Saul family remained in West Haddon for many years but eventually moved to another part of the Midlands where Robert Saul died in 1983 when he was 75 years old.

While talking to people about their experiences and recollections of the incident, I have come across several strange coincidences which link together individuals from the community where PB 304 crashed, and members of its crew. One concerns a Mrs Gladys Keever who witnessed the Lancaster flying perilously close to the steeple of St.George's Church and being quite young at the time was so shocked

145

by what happened that her mother decided to send her away for a while until things got back to normal. Having an aunt living near Wolverhampton she went to stay with her and a week or so after her arrival, she and the family were watching a funeral procession going past, when it stopped immediately outside their window. The coffin was draped with a Union Jack so everyone guessed the deceased was a serviceman and when someone in Gladys' family made inquiries they were astounded to discover it was the funeral of Sergeant John Davenport. Having travelled a considerable distance (by wartime standards) to forget about the horrors of what had happened in Salford, they now found themselves in the middle of the mourning for one of the Salford victims - in Sedgeley.

It is claimed that as the aircraft passed close to Halton Bank, a cousin of Sergeant Barnes the flight engineer saw it and said, "That's our Raymond!" Edith Ridley later moved to Leicestershire and died in 1987 but her husband said he will never forget that Sunday morning when his wife looked up and made the statement with an unusual certainty in her voice. There is no logical explanation for such a premonition, but with the crew experiencing high emotional states of anxiety as their stricken aircraft made its approach, who is to say what unseen forces were at work.

At the outbreak of war my father was 30 years old but not eligible for active service because of a badly damaged right arm, which had been broken several times. Both his elder brother Frank and his younger brother Ernie were in the army serving in the Far East and my father must have felt he wanted to do his bit and so he joined the ARP. He became a part-time warden in April 1940 serving throughout the worst of the blitz on Manchester and Salford and ultimately was established as a full-time warden in October 1941 when he worked out of Post "X3" in Colwyn Street Seedley. It is an interesting window on the times that acceptance for service with the ARP was not simply a matter of being available and competition between applicants was engendered as a result of what were then considered to be quite good rates of pay. By 1944 full-time male wardens were earning £4.6.0. per week and their female counterparts £2.12.0. - the concept of equal pay would have been considered ludicrous if not obscene in those days of male superiority.

In April 1944 my family received news that my Uncle Frank had been killed, while serving as a medic with The Lancashire Fusiliers in Burma. My grandmother, Lucy Bamford, was in poor health at the time so everyone agreed not to inform her of Frank's death until she got stronger but this well intentioned pact was defeated one night when my father arrived home and whilst visiting his mother, had found out that she already knew of Frank's death. Running downstairs he had accused his sisters, Alice and Lillian, of telling their mother about the telegram which they had energetically denied and after a row all three had gone upstairs to ask her how she knew. Grandmother confirmed she did not know about a telegram and no one had said anything, but Frank together with Edith and John, had visited her.

Edith had died in 1923, and John after a mining accident in 1930 but with quiet conviction the old lady related how all three had stood at the bottom of her bed and Frank had told her what had happened. According to my father she knew certain details of his death that were not given in the telegram, nor in the official letter that followed. Frank was 39 years old, an experienced professional soldier who left a widow and two children. Lucy had struggled alone to bring up Frank, as indeed all of her children since her husband, John William, had died in January 1916 and the loss of another son was probably the beginning of the end, although she was a strong willed woman and would not have given up her life easily.

For the last few years of her life my grandmother was under the care of a Doctor D.H. Fraser of Broad Street Pendleton and at the inquest into her death, held at Pendleton Town Hall on Wednesday 16 August, Doctor Fraser told the Coroner that my grandmother had received medical attention for four years, after being taken ill with a heart condition. My father informed the inquest that his mother was sleeping downstairs because of her illness and when the aircraft crashed, he ran downstairs but found the window and window-frame blown in and his mother covered in blood. As I have previously recorded however, despite severe cuts to her neck and arms she did not want to stay in hospital and continually demanded to be allowed home. Because of the severe damage to the properties along Langley Road that was not possible so Lucy was taken to her daughter's home where she later died.

With Langley Road having its own football and cricket teams several well known footballers were brought up in the area including Geoff Bent, a local lad who played for Manchester United and who was killed in the Munich air crash in 1958. My father knew the family and I remember him taking me round to see his mother, who then lived at Irlam O'th Height. Ira Winstanley, who played for Stoke City with Stanley Matthews also came from the area and many years later in the 1960s, he returned to Pendlebury and took over The Butcher's Arms

147

public house on Bolton Road, from the Potts family. Sport was an important activity in maintaining links amongst the Langley Road and Whit Lane communities and, with Littleton Road Playing Fields just across the river, access to the necessary space was no problem. Amongst those who played regularly before the war were Walter Grundy, Walter Rushton, my father and Johnny Barnes.

After being in hospital for 13 weeks Johnny Barnes eventually regained a small amount of sight, wore a green shade over his eyes for a time and attended the hospital every day for five years before the doctors would discharge him. In spite of all his years of suffering he still had to go before a medical board who certified Johnny as 80% blind, allowing him to claim a small pension. The little sight which remained progressively disappeared over the years until finally Johnny was confirmed as being 100% blind. Eva Barnes returned to her home some eight weeks after the Lancaster crashed and when Johnny came out of hospital they moved to a larger house just around the corner in Dixon Street, in fact the house where Mary Hassall lived, and from where she witnessed the Lancaster's final moments. John and Eva have a large family, four boys and two girls who needed the extra rooms, as Johnny's mother also lived with them. At the time of writing they are the only survivors who remain in the community.

The other Barnes family, that of the flight engineer, Sergeant Raymond Barnes, lived in a pit cottage on Bolton Road until they were bombed out during the blitz. In Gladstone Street, very close to where they lived a 500 kg air mine exploded and several people were killed. Raymond's parents and his younger sister moved into West Drive on the Temple Lodge Estate. This part of town did not escape being hit by German bombs either but genrally the raids there were not as heavy. On 28 April, 1953, Raymond's family came close to being involved in a disaster when three houses in an adjacent street, Temple Drive, fell into a construction shaft of the disused 1,299 yard long "Black Harry" Railway Tunnel. Five people died and two more were very lucky to be rescued. Raymond's mother Dorothy, died in 1963, never having fully recovered from the loss of her son. His father Harold Barnes died a few years later. Irene is the sole survivor of the family. Having been married for many years she and her husband Bill have three daughters and several grandchildren.

In July 1968 I joined the Royal Air Force and the origins of my motivation for writing this book undoubtably go back to that period. In the control tower at RAF Manston where I served between 1968-71, I worked beside several airmen who having flown during the war were by the late 60s in their final years with the RAF. Master Engineer Burns; Master Pilot Brown; Flight Sergeant Kay and Flight Lieutenant Winters are just a few of their names; the latter having flown Hurricanes in the early stages of the war, later flew Wellingtons and Liberators but died of pleurisy over the Easter of 1969.

Senior Aircraftsman Hughy O'Neil, another survivor from the war regularly used to talk of the carnage at Manston in 1944. He described scenes of bombers crashing and being bulldozed off the runway as soon as the survivors had been dragged out, before the next Lancaster or Halifax landed. The bodies of the dead were left in the wreckage to be recovered later. Hughy had been affected by what he had seen and he would often shout at me, claiming that I had no idea what it was like then.

The strength of the Royal Air Force peaked in October 1944 with 1,171, 421 personnel under its control but after the war huge reductions in manpower took place and by 1947, the majority of those who served through the hostilities had been demobbed. Those individuals who did sign on as regulars were normally reduced in rank though others continued to fly with the RAF Volunteer Reserve. Immediately after the war many former airmen were either too busy with families and work to re-unite with their old crews but in more recent years various organizations have sprung up to provide comradeship and support. The Aircrew Association, Bomber Command Association and The Royal Air Force Association all provide opportunities for former airmen to meet, reminisce about their shared experiences, or trace their former crew members. Squadron reunions, organized by the respective squadron associations also play a great role in keeping everyone in touch and provide invaluable links.

It was at the 1991 Reunion 106 Squadron that I had the good fortune to meet three of the crew from PB 248, Syd Geater, Don Hodges and Ron Pattison, part of a crew which Syd nicknamed the Scallywags, during a visit to the Lincolnshire Aviation Heritage Centre at East Kirby. In October that year Syd and Don flew over to Canada to reunite with the rest of their crew who live in Toronto although their former flight engineer, Ron Pattison, was now an unavoidable absentee, being unfit to travel after suffering a stroke. In 1992 they held another reunion in Canada but this time it was a more sombre affair as former Flying Officer Mitchell, the bomb aimer, had died suddenly.

By 1993 the health of Ron Pattison had deteriorated and Don Merideth flew over from Canada to see him - which for the former pilot was a gesture requiring particular determination since after the war he had decided never to fly again. It seemed strange that after all the dangerous missions he had been on, something made him not want to fly, but wartime experiences affected everyone in different ways. The surviving members of the crew keep in touch however and more reunions are planned for the future.

Former Warrant Officer Jim Cunningham died on 20 December, 1991, after being ill for some time with a heart condition. For several years after leaving the RAF he flew Chipmunks with an Air Experience Flight near his home in Edinburgh and in his later years enjoyed breeding tropical fish as a hobby. Jim left behind a wife and two children, although his wife died soon after her husband, his son John, lives in Scotland and his married daughter Elizabeth is married and now resides in Ontario Canada. Both are very proud of their father's service in the RAF and have been very helpful to me in my research.

He is survived by several of his old crew including the navigator Bill Hovey, Cecil Lawlan the flight engineer and Derek Whiting his rear gunner. After his tour on 106 Squadron Derek went to 17 OTU at Silverstone as an instructor and later served on 617 Squadron and 83 Squadron. The crew never had a reunion as such, but kept in touch through writing to each other and by conversations on the telephone. Bill Hovey could not recall Peter Lines or his crew, but remembered Sergeant Singh who was a well known character in the sergeants' mess and had a reputation for being something of a ladies' man!

New Zealander Arthur Kitto returned to his native country after the war but kept in touch with some of his old friends from 106 Squadron. In 1995 he wrote to me explaining how he and his crew nearly came to a sticky end after overshooting his wireless operator's home in Haworth, while on a training flight. On the first pass he made a mess of things and had to go around again but the second approach was also very dicey and he reckoned he may have loosened a number of roof tiles as his Lancaster roared overhead. Since then he has not returned to Bronte Country but claimed that many of the older residents in the town will never forget a certain day in 1944 when they might have thought their world was coming to a sudden and premature end!

Former Flight Lieutenant Peter Perry who flew with 106 through the winter of 1943-44 and the man who taught Flight Lieutenant Lines to fly the Lancaster, later flew Avro Yorks but unfortunately after suffering a problem with one of his eyes was grounded and subsequently trained as an air traffic controller. In 1973 when I returned to Britain from Cyprus, I was originally posted to Preston Air Traffic Control Centre at Barton Hall but at the last minute it was changed and I was sent back to Manston in Kent. Had I gone to Preston I would certainly have met Peter Perry because he was then the Senior Air Traffic Control Officer. As it happened our meeting was delayed until 1991, when Peter got in touch by responding to my letter which appeared in *Air Mail* appealing for help - so it seems we were destined to meet at one time or another. Peter went on to become the Senior Air Traffic Controller at Manchester Airport, reaching the top of his profession. He is now retired but remains an active member of the 106 Squadron Association and The Aircrew Association.

At the time of writing, several of the people who lived on Langley Road and Whit Lane in 1944 remain in the Salford area, including Mary Wardle, Joyce Bowles and Albert Phillip. Others like Harriet Chase, who was dug out of the remains of her home, did not survive very long after the incident and she died on 7 November, 1946, when she was 63 years old. My father, Joseph, who provided the spark which first kindled my determination to chronicle these events, died on 2 February, 1992, aged 83 years having worked at Ward and Goldstones on Frederick Road Salford for over twenty five years, until his retirement in 1974. Hugh Yates who in 1944 was an ARP messenger, later served in The Royal Navy and he died on 5 October 1993, aged only 59 years.

On Remembrance Sunday 1991, Albert Phillips, together with Tom Donnolly and Ray Griffiths of the Manchester Branch of The Aircrew Association, laid flowers on the crash site. It was a terribly wet day but a very special one, because it was the first time any kind of commemorative ceremony had been held there since the late 1940s. In 1992 with the co-operation of St.George's Church and The Reverend David Knight, a service was held on the crash site and prayers read for those who died. On this occasion former Sergeant Syd Geater attended the ceremony and proudly represented 106 Squadron.

In July 1991 The Salford Lancaster Memorial Appeal was launched with the aim of raising sufficient funds to erect a Commemorative Memorial to honour the seven airmen of Lancaster PB 304. Those who have attended its meetings and helped to raise funds include Joyce Bowles, Helen Lomas and Irene Barnes, the sister of the flight engineer, as well as Bob Howie and Albert Bracegirdle who both served on 106 Squadron. The Salford Royal Air Force Association and Boothstown British Legion Club have helped enormously, as have individuals such as Ray Leech, Ken McNee, Walter Magee, and Cyril George the treasurer. Contributions also include generous donations from George Morris, Hazel Boardman and the late Hugh Yates. None

151

of it would have been possible though without the help and co-operation of my long suffering partner Janice Saunders, who provided ideas and support when things went wrong.

On 30 July, 1994, exactly fifty years after the tragedy happened, a Memorial was dedicated to the seven airmen, in Agecroft Cemetery only a short distance away from where the seven airmen died. The service was held by The Reverend David Knight of St. George's Church and attended by Councillor Vincent Price, The Mayor of Salford. Former Flight Lieutenant Peter Perry and Sergeant Syd Geater proudly represented 106 Squadron. The cadets of 1099 Squadron Air Training Corps (Worsley) were also in attendance and under the command of Flight Lieutenant Snowdon provided a Guard of Honour worthy of the occasion.

The final tribute was paid by the Royal Air Force, when at 1330 hours and exactly on time, Lancaster PA 474, from The Battle of Britain Memorial Flight at Coningsby performed a flypast. The sound of its Merlin engines made many a heart flutter and for those who had been around in July 1944 evocative memories came flooding back providing the perfect way to end the service.